PEOPLE STUDYING PEOPLE

PEOPLE STUDYING PEOPLE

THE HUMAN ELEMENT IN FIELDWORK

Robert A. Georges
and
Michael O. Jones

UNIVERSITY OF CALIFORNIA PRESS
Berkeley • Los Angeles • London

University of California Press
Berkeley and Los Angeles, California

University of California Press, Ltd.
London, England

5 6 7 8 9 0

Library of Congress Cataloging in Publication Data

Georges, Robert A.
    People studying people.

    Includes bibliographical references and index.
    1. Social sciences—Field work.   2. Interpersonal relations.
I. Jones, Michael Owen, joint author.   II. Title.
H62.G46   001.4'3   79-65767

ISBN 0-520-04067-8 (alk. paper)

Printed in the United States of America

The paper used in this publication meets the minimum requirements
of American National Standard for Information Sciences—Permanence of
Paper for Printed Library Materials, ANSI Z39.48–1984. ⊗

For
Mary and Jon
and
Jane and David

Contents

Prologue

The meaning of the word *fieldwork* is changing. Once referring to laborious agricultural tasks performed by hand, it has come to designate the act of inquiring into the nature of phenomena by studying them at first hand in the environments in which they naturally exist or occur. It is this meaning that is most often implied or intended when *fieldwork* is used by those who make human beings the subjects of their investigations.

Long associated with the activities of the folklorist, anthropologist, linguist, and sociologist, fieldwork now attracts the psychologist, artist, ethnomusicologist, educator, historian, and student of dance and theater. Courses in fieldwork have proliferated in colleges and universities, and they are often an integral part of training programs for military and law enforcement personnel. In the minds of some, doing fieldwork has become synonymous with conducting research. It is a required ritual for many people seeking academic degrees or aspiring to positions in public service. It is even prerequisite to employment and advancement in selected professions.

This growing emphasis on fieldwork in the arts, humanities, and social sciences has been paralleled by the publication of an increasing number of books and articles on the subject. Most of these are addressed to prospective fieldworkers trained in a specific discipline rather than to seasoned researchers. Often structured as guides or manuals, they present sets of procedures intended to lead the uninitiated step by step from planning to reporting stages, or they dwell upon specific problems or aspects of the endeavor, such as ways to sample a population or to conduct an interview. Principal topics consist of the kinds of data to elicit and the ways to record, analyze, and present them. Two things are implied. One is that a fieldworker's goal is to get information. The other is that to achieve this goal there is a logical method that can be mastered and must be followed.

Getting information, of course, is a primary reason for engaging in fieldwork. One expects to learn, whether one records the customs of exotic peoples or scrutinizes the habits of one's peers, observes the pirouette of a ballet dancer, or notes the way in which a country craftsman assembles a chair. What is learned necessarily serves as the source of information reported to others. Fieldwork requiring people to study other people at first hand, however, entails much more than merely knowing what to observe and how to record, process, and present it. The fieldworker must explain his or her presence and purpose to others, gain their confidence and cooperation, and develop and maintain mutually acceptable relationships. These requirements create dilemmas, produce confrontations, demand clarifications and compromises, and evoke reflection and introspection that one can neither fully anticipate nor prepare for in advance. Worthwhile projects may fail. Research strategies frequently must be modified or abandoned as researchers and subjects interact. Unexpected opportunities, fruitful leads, and important insights can blossom as fieldwork develops. Planning for fieldwork enables the researcher to project the means of achieving envisioned ends, but the personal nature of the experience and the response of individuals determine the results and the true significance of the pursuit.

Those who have written about fieldwork in recent years have begun to include remarks concerning the human and personal nature of the enterprise. Descriptions of fieldworkers' squalid living conditions and of hostile informants dispel romantic notions of idyllic field sites and friendly natives. Recently published diaries, letters, and reminiscences of early twentieth-century fieldworkers reveal that data presented in many field-based studies now considered classics were often obtained under conditions that can hardly be regarded as systematic or scientific. Coping with problems created by feelings of loneliness, alienation, and frustration, it is now apparent, is as demanding and difficult for the fieldworker as are the tasks of conducting interviews or observing and documenting behavior.

While personal problems generated in fieldwork are considered worthy of discussion and examination today, most fieldworkers treat them apart from, rather than as a part of, their reports. Mentioned in passing, usually in appendixes or occasionally in introductions to published works, are difficulties that arise as fieldworkers attempt to communicate their purpose and comply with the unwritten rules of research populations. Tensions created by uncertainties about the effects of the fieldworker's presence upon the future well-being of individuals or groups are described in footnotes or in digressive sentences, if at all. The information obtained, rather than the experience lived, remains the focus of most field-based studies.

There is an obvious correlation between information gathered firsthand and the contexts in which that information is elicited and provided. A subject's response to the fieldworker's questions about most topics is determined by expectations of what the fieldworker wants to know and why she or he wishes that information. One whose motives are suspect may meet a chilly silence by asking questions about esoteric rituals. Conversely, information about intimate practices may be volunteered by those who regard the fieldworker as being sincerely interested in their behavior. Regardless of the topic, the ways in which the fieldworker raises an issue and frames questions will also strike the subject as significant. Direct queries may be abrasive to some but demanded by others, and questioning of any kind might be inappropriate in particular situations.

In this work we trace the threads of personal relations between researchers and their subjects out of which the fabric of fieldwork is woven. Our basic premise is that an understanding of fieldwork is dependent upon an appreciation for the fundamental human nature of the pursuit. However else they may identify themselves and each other, fieldworker and subject are first and foremost human beings. It is this shared identity that makes fieldwork, with both its problems and its accomplishments, a meaningful mode of mutual learning.

Dilemmas

O ne morning . . . the old chief appeared graver and more affectionate toward me than usual," notes a field-worker in a report of his experiences trying to document customs. "He told me the *'Ho-mah-tchi* was coming—a very *sa-mu* (ill-natured) dance,' and suggested that 'it would be well for me not to sketch it.'" Unaware that a council had ordered the Knife Dance to put an end to his objectionable behavior, the researcher persisted. Vexed, the man who had befriended him exclaimed, " 'Oh, well, of course, a fool always makes a fool of himself.'" The warning was shrugged off.[1]

"When the great dance appeared, the governor seemed desirous of keeping me at home. During most of the morning I humored him in this," writes the fieldworker. "At last, however, fearing I would miss some important ceremonial, I stole out across the house-tops and took a position on one of the terraces of the dance court." He describes what he saw. "The dancers filed in through the covered way, preceded by a priest, and arranged themselves in a line across the court. Their costumes were not unlike those of the first dance I had witnessed, save that the masks were flatter and smeared with blood, and the beards and hair were long and streaming." He continues, "In their right hands the performers carried huge, leaf-shaped, blood-stained knives of stone, which, during the movements of the dance, they brandished wildly in the air, in time and accompaniment to their wild song and regular steps, often pointing them toward me." As the day advanced, spectators thronged the terrace; most of them shied away from the fieldworker, however, who busied himself with note-taking and sketching.[2]

Suddenly two characters dashed into the court. Adorned in skull caps, painted with ashes, sporting around the neck a twisted rope of black fiber, and wielding war-clubs, they made a ghastly sight. Their harangues at each other were initially greeted with laughter, but before long even the children became silent.

"Soon they began to point wildly at me with their clubs," writes the fieldworker. "Unable as I was to understand all they had been saying, I at first regarded it all as a joke," he notes, "until one shouted out to the other, 'Kill him! Kill him!' and the women and children excitedly rising rushed for the door-ways or gathered closer to one another." At that moment the larger man brandished his club at the observer, violently striking the ladder near the top of which the researcher was sitting, and began to climb. "A few Indians had collected behind me, and a host of them stood all around in front. Therefore, I realized that in case of violence, escape would be impossible," observes the fieldworker, describing his reaction.[3]

"I forced a laugh," he writes, "quickly drew my hunting-knife from the bottom of the pouch, waved it two or three times in the air so that it flashed in the sunlight, and laid it conspicuously in front of me." He describes his behavior further. "Still smiling, I carefully placed my book—open—by the side of the pouch and laid a stone on it to show that I intended to resume the sketching. Then I half rose, clinging to the ladder-pole with one hand, and holding the other in readiness to clutch the knife." He indicates the men's reactions. "The one below suddenly grabbed the skirt of the other and shouted, 'Hold on, he is a *kí-he!* a *kí-he!* We have been mistaken. This is no Navajo.' Jumping down to the ground," reports the writer, "the one thus addressed glanced up at me for an instant, waved his war-club in the air, breathed from it, and echoed the words of his companion, while the spectators wildly shouted applause." The fieldworker was, they had finally decided, a "spiritual friend," one endowed with sacred powers for the good of mankind. "The two held a hurried conference. They swore they must 'kill a Navajo,' and dashed through the crowd and passage-way out of the court.'"[4]

The fieldworker stayed put. "As I replaced my knife and resumed the sketching, the eyes of nearly the whole assemblage were turned toward me, and the applause, mingled with loud remarks, was redoubled," he writes. "Some of the old men even came up and patted me on the head, or breathed on my hands and from their own." But the episode was not yet over.[5]

"Presently a prolonged howl outside the court attracted the attention of all, and the frantic pair rushed in through the covered way, dragging by the tail and hind legs a big, yelping, snapping, shaggy yellow dog," continues the fieldworker, recounting more details about the incident. "'We have found a Navajo,' exclaimed one, as they threw the dog violently against the ground." While the dog was cringing before the two men, "they began an erratic dance, wildly gesticulating and brandishing their clubs, and interjecting their snatches of song with short speeches. Suddenly, one of them struck the brute across the muzzle with his war-club, and a well-directed blow from the other broke its back," reports the observer. "While it was yet gasping and struggling, the smaller one of the two rushed about frantically yelling, 'A knife, a knife.' One was thrown down to him. Snatching it up, he grabbed the animal and made a gash in its viscera."[6]

The scene that followed is not described, for it was "too disgusting." Instead, the fieldworker sums up the experience and interprets the event. "Whether the Indians had really designed to murder me, or merely to intimidate me," he writes, "my coolness, as well as my waving of the knife toward the sun, both largely accidental, had made a great impression on them. For never afterward was I molested to any serious extent in attempting to make notes and sketches." There were immediate results as well. "That night," writes the fieldworker, "the old chief was profuse in his congratulations and words of praise. I had completed in him, that day, the winning of the truest of friends; and by so doing had decided the fate of my mission among the Zuñi Indians."[7]

Why was Frank Hamilton Cushing, the author of these words, among the Zuni? What did he want? How did he proceed? Perhaps more important, what are some of the implications of Cushing's experiences and the ramifications of his sketch for fieldworkers and the people they study today?

Cushing's account of his fieldwork experiences appeared in

serial form in *The Century Magazine* in 1882 and 1883 under the title "My Adventures in Zuñi." The vignette is a rarity. Despite the myriad collections of field data and reports of observations, as well as the innumerable analyses based on field-work, little is known about the particular ways in which field-workers obtained information. Was it elicited or volunteered? How did the researchers conceive of the people whose behavior they studied? How did the people whose behavior was observed identify and respond to the researchers? How did these identities and relationships shape the outcome of the investigations?[8] "We have to turn our attention first of all to the artist himself," writes Franz Boas in his discussion of North American Indian art. Boas in fact was unable to comply with his own demand because "unfortunately," he admits, "observations on this subject are very rare and unsatisfactory, for it requires an intimate knowledge of the people to understand the innermost thought and feelings of the artist."[9] Boas depended largely on objects rather than people as the basis for his inferences about North American Indian art, as others have restricted their examinations to the basic plots of narratives in their discussions of storytelling. Ruth Benedict, who trusted interpreters (but who never identifies them, explains how they were chosen, or indicates their role in her investigations) implies in her writings that she had probed the minds and actions of individuals in order to determine the functions of customs and the dynamic nature of the art of taletelling,[10] but evaluation of her work is difficult without knowledge of her methods.

Melville and Frances Herskovits recorded Dahomean narratives in their hotel room; because of an imperfect knowledge of the native language, they were forced to use interpreters and then had to translate the narratives from French into English as they typed the texts.[11] Colin Turnbull was contemptuous of the Ik, whom he decided to study only because political unrest in the Congo and the Indian government's refusal of permission made it impossible for him to work among the peoples of Ituri Forest and the Andaman Islands, respectively.[12] William Hugh Jansen, when collecting stories in Kentucky, mentioned to his landlady that a man he had just met told him some "old-time tales," suggesting that this was an admirable thing to do, thereby prompting her for leads to other storytellers. Her response was, "Old-time tales nothing. All he tells are lies."[13] Several of

John Dollard's informants challenged him, questioning his motives for coming to the South to study black-white relations, doubting the validity of his methods in carrying out the research, and assailing his interpretations of their behavior.[14] In Levittown, Pennsylvania, Herbert Gans concealed from many people the fact that he was a sociologist, sometimes claiming to be an historian and at other times identifying himself simply as a resident and a neighbor; this selective revelation of purpose and identity produced some unexpected results, among which was a feeling of guilt about the prospects of reporting certain kinds of information.[15] Nevertheless, these and other researchers have persevered, creating for us ethnographies and collections of information about the people they have studied. But what effects have the conditions of fieldwork had upon that which has been reported?

Cushing's characterization of his fieldwork experiences among the Zuni is unusual in another way. It contrasts sharply with the image generated in treatises on fieldwork and by most ethnographies; namely, that research is always well planned and systematic and that events go smoothly. Fieldwork guides tend to leave the impression that the logic of inquiry, which the authors have reconstructed, is the same as logic-in-use. Research is presented as largely a matter of stating what one is interested in, determining how to learn more about that topic, and then filling in the gaps in one's knowledge and understanding by making some observations or by interviewing people.[16] Once observational skills and record-making techniques are mastered, one is presumably equipped to go "into the field." According to the authors of some manuals, even amateurs and Sunday collectors can do fieldwork, an important task which, they imply, is not too difficult, is often exciting, and is sometimes fun.[17] There are, however, many unplanned events in conducting fieldwork for which one is not really prepared, nor is one assisted in most of the available literature in dealing with the personal element inherent in this type of research requiring firsthand interaction with other people.

Cushing's fieldwork experiences exemplify many of these problems. Consider the circumstances that led to his sojourn among the Zuni. "One hot summer day in 1879," he writes, "as I was sitting in my office in the ivy-mantled old South Tower of the Smithsonian Institution, a messenger boy tapped at my door, and said: 'Professor Baird wishes to see you, sir.' " Cushing continues his account. "The Professor, picking up his umbrellas and papers, came toward the door as I entered. 'Haven't I heard you say you would like to go to New Mexico to study the cliff-houses and Pueblo Indians?' " Baird asked Cushing. Cushing's response was immediate: " 'Yes, sir.' " He reports Baird's next question. " 'Would you still like to go?' " Again, the answer was positive. " 'Yes, sir.' " Cushing quotes the professor's instructions. " 'Very well then, be ready to accompany Colonel Stevenson's collecting party, as ethnologist, within four days. I want you to find out all you can about some typical tribe of Pueblo Indians. Make your own choice of field, and use your own methods; only, get the information,' " commanded Baird. " 'You will probably be gone three months. Write me frequently. I'm in a hurry this evening. Look to Major Powell, of the Bureau of Ethnology, if you want further directions. Good-day.' " Cushing notes the outcome of this interview. "Thus it happened that, on a sultry afternoon in late September, by no means firmly seated in the first saddle I had ever bestridden, I was belaboring a lazy Government mule just at the entrance of a pass between two great banded red-and-gray sandstone mesas, in the midst of a waterless wilderness."[18]

Students will recognize some elements in Cushing's experiences similar to their own. They walk into a classroom and learn that to receive a passing grade in the course they must do fieldwork and submit a written report discussing the results. They probably will be given some instruction in how to observe and make records, particularly if the course has the word *fieldwork* in its title; but to a great extent they will be left to their own devices. "Get the information!" they will be told.

According to Cushing's account, his trip to New Mexico (on the basis of which he obtained information for many publications and earned a reputation as a pioneering and perceptive ethnologist) was a matter of happenstance. Chance also has been responsible for the decisions of many others to study certain behaviors, peoples, or events. Bronislaw Malinowski's sojourn in the Trobriand Islands seemed to have resulted in part because of the consequences of Europe at war. Since he was an alien in residence in England, it was considered judicious for all concerned that he remain out of the country for the duration of the conflict.[19] When those carrying their supplies deserted

Margaret Mead and Reo Fortune near a mountain village in New Guinea, the two anthropologists could not proceed to their preplanned field destination. They acquiesced and studied instead the only accessible population, the Mountain Arapesh.[20] Henry Glassie went to Northern Ireland with the intent of preparing an ethnography describing how residents managed their daily affairs amid political strife. When talking one evening to an elderly woman about Christmas customs, however, he learned that some of the older men in the area had once been mummers; excited, Glassie changed topics and recorded information about the drama which he subsequently published.[21] Others have had topics or problems, behaviors or peoples, suggested to them by instructors, colleagues, and chance acquaintances. Sometimes careers have been built, or lives destroyed, as a result.

Cushing might have been killed doing fieldwork; Raymond Kennedy was; Michael Clark Rockefeller may have been (though his fate remains a mystery). Others have contracted malaria, hepatitis, or dysentery. Some have been temporarily or permanently disabled. In at least one instance, the child of a fieldworker died shortly after the family arrived at the fieldwork site.[22] For the most part, however, such nightmares go unreported.

Students today have an advantage over Cushing. They can take courses in fieldwork: indeed, they are often compelled to do so. They can read handbooks that assist them in writing a proposal or that instruct them in interviewing, administering questionnaires, tape-recording, taking photographs, or making films. Furthermore, they can learn from the insights and profit from the mistakes of those who have preceded them. It is sometimes remarked by students and professionals that after their most recent fieldwork experiences, they realized how ill prepared they were for the task. Despite their knowledge and training, they still had to rely on their own methods, as Cushing did.

What were Cushing's methods? Were they entirely accidental? Was he not prepared at all for his encounters in the field? Obviously, he could take notes and draw. "I had been busy with memoranda and had succeeded in sketching three or four of the costumes," he informs us.[23] He also suggests that he was capable of preparing himself experientially as events occurred.

The first Indian that Cushing met as he descended from a canyon rim happened to be a Zuni, though Cushing did not at first know it. Neither man could understand the other. When the Indian extended his hand, Cushing shook it warmly and asked, "Zuñi?" The Indian was ecstatic and reverentially breathed on Cushing's hand from his own, nodding toward the smoky terraces in the distance.[24] Absorbed in watching a dance on one of the plazas, none of the three-hundred Zuni noticed Cushing until he was virtually upon them. Suddenly, he was confronted by forty or fifty men. Cushing writes, "One of them approached and spoke something in Spanish, motioning me away; but I did not understand him, so I grasped his hand and breathed on it as I had seen the herder do. Lucky thought! The old man was pleased," observes Cushing. He explains the results of his act, noting that the man, smiling, "hastily addressed the others, who, after watching me with approving curiosity, gathered around to shake hands and exchange breaths, until I might have regarded myself as President."[25]

Cushing used other techniques to ingratiate himself. Observing that the men usually smoked when they gathered to discuss matters, Cushing often provided the cigarettes and, though a nonsmoker himself, he also lit up. When he sketched, he always showed his subjects the drawings. "They were wonder-struck, and would pass their fingers over the figures as though they expected to feel them." Yet despite their interest, the Zuni objected strenuously when Cushing attempted to sketch their dances. To conciliate them, he began to carry sugar and trinkets with which he tempted the children. "I grew in their favor, and within a few days had a crowd of them always at my heels. The parents were delighted, and began to share the affection of their children. Nevertheless, the next time I sketched a dance, all this went for nothing."[26]

Discouraged, Cushing decided to try to live with the Indians, so he moved his belongings into the governor's house. Cushing, like many subsequent fieldworkers, envisioned such an action as a means of learning about a people by participating more directly in their activities. But what were the consequences of this unilateral decision? "When the old chief came in that evening and saw that I had made myself at home, he shrugged his shoulders," writes Cushing, whose report of the man's first question suggests that the governor was not too pleased. " 'How

long will it be before you go back to Washington?' he attempted
to ask." Cushing replied that it would be perhaps two months
before he was to leave the area, and hence the governor's home.
" 'Tuh!' (damn) was his only exclamation as he climbed to the
roof and disappeared through the sky-hole," Cushing reports.[27]

As Cushing settled in, he became acquainted with the governor's family. He notes that it "consisted of the governor's ugly
wife, a short-statured, large-mouthed, slant-eyed, bushy-haired
hypochondriac, yet the soul of obedience to her husband, and
ultimately of kindness to me, for she conceived a violent fancy
for me, because I petted her noisy, dirty, and adored little niece.
Not so was her old aunt," who regarded Cushing "as though I
were a wizard, or a persistent nightmare." The governor
despised her almost as much as he disliked her nephew, whose
wife he called "a bag of hard howls." The governor's brother-
in-law was "a short, rather thick and greasy man, excessively
conceited, ignorant, narrow," whom the chief nicknamed
"Who-talks-himself-dry." Others in the family were as offen-
sive to Cushing as he was to them at first, and as they were to
one another.[28] "I made fair progress in the good graces of this
odd group," claims Cushing, "but still by them, as by the rest
of the tribe, I was regarded as a sort of black sheep on account
of my sketching and note-taking, and suspicions seemed to
increase in proportion to the evident liking they began to have
for me."[29]

Cushing was determined not to abandon the pursuit. Because
of his persistence, a grave council was held. It occurred in the
same room in which he slept; "as I lay in my hammock listening
to the proceedings," he writes, "the discussion grew louder and
more and more excited, the subjects evidently being my papers
and myself." After the council broke up, "the governor
approached me, candle in hand, and intently regarded my face
for several minutes." Cushing reports what the governor said to
him. " 'The *Keá-k'ok-shi* (Sacred Dance) is coming to-morrow.
What think you?' " Cushing's reply ignored the gravity of the
situation. " 'I think it will rain.' " The governor responded in
the following way, " 'And *I* think,' said he, as he set his mouth
and glared at me with his black eyes, 'that you will not see the
Keá-k'ok-shi when it comes to-morrow.' " Undaunted, Cushing said, " '*I* think I *shall*. . . .' "[30] Cushing was indeed on hand
for the dance. He was warned to put aside his books and pen-

cils. "I must carry them wherever I go," he insisted,[31] and most of the time he did.

Cushing's determination to "get the information," and his success in doing so, motivated him to ask permission to extend his stay among the Zuni. His request was approved by the Smithsonian Institution, so he broached the subject with the Zuni governor, giving what he felt would be acceptable reasons. "I told the governor that Washington wished me to remain there some months longer, to write all about his children, the Zuñis, and to sketch their dances and dresses," reports Cushing, who notes the governor's response. " 'Hai!' said the old man. 'Why does Washington want to know about our Kâ-kâ? The Zuñis have their religion and the Americans have theirs.' " In continuing his account, Cushing suggests that he flattered the governor as a potential contributor to better Anglo-Indian relations, for he writes that he asked the governor, " 'Do you want Washington to be a friend of the Zuñis? How can you expect a people to like others without knowing something about them? Some fools and bad men have said "the Zuñis have no religion." It is because they are always saying such things of some Indians, that we do not understand them. Hence, instead of all being brothers, we fight.' "[32]

Cushing's strategy seemed successful, for he was permitted to remain. Yet before the members of the Smithsonian party that had come for him had departed, Cushing became aware of the fact that his remaining would entail his making a number of concessions. The governor snatched off Cushing's helmet and bound his head with a long, black silken scarf. He insisted that Cushing wear a pair of buckskin moccasins instead of the "squeaking foot-packs," as the governor called his English walking shoes. "Thus, in a blue flannel shirt, corduroy breeches, long canvas leggings, Zuñi moccasins, and head-band, heartily ashamed of my mongrel costume, I had to walk across the whole pueblo and down to camp, the old man peering proudly around the corner of an eagle-cage at me as I started," writes Cushing. He describes the conflicting responses to his dress and notes his reaction. "The Zuñis greeted me enthusiastically, but when I reached camp great game was made of me. I returned thoroughly disgusted, determined never to wear the head-band again; but, when I looked for the hat and shoes, they were nowhere to be found."[33]

In the days that followed, more of Cushing's garb was taken from him and exchanged for Zuni clothing. He was forced to eat Zuni food. Even his hammock was torn down, and he was required to sleep on the floor on sheepskins as his hosts did. "I want to make a Zuñi of you," said the chief.[34] Once begun, the transformation of Cushing continued unabated. "My foster father, and many other of the principal men of the tribe, now insisted that my ears be pierced," writes Cushing. "I steadily refused; but they persisted, until at last it occurred to me that there must be some meaning in their urgency, and I determined to yield to their request." At the ceremony, Cushing was given a new name, that of *Té-na-tsa-li*, 'Medicine Flower' (he had often dispensed salves and ointments), signaling his growing acceptance by the Zunis.[35]

There was still the matter of his not having taken a woman. One was thrust upon him. Cushing tried to ignore her attentions, but to no avail. There seemed to be only one solution. "I left word for her to come and eat with me at sunset. When she came, I was writing. She was accompanied by her aunt. I bade them enter, set coffee, bread, *he-we* [corn cakes, made by the girl] sugar, and other delicacies before them," Cushing reports. "Then I merely broke a crust, sacrificed some of it to the fire, ate a mouthful, and left them, resuming my writing." Cushing describes the effects of his acts. "The girl dropped her half-eaten bread, threw her head-mantle over her face, and started for the door. I called to her and offered a bag of sugar in payment, I said, for the *he-we*. At first she angrily refused; then bethinking herself that I was an American and possibly knew no better, she took the sugar and hastened away, mortified and almost ready to cry with vexation." Cushing characterizes his own feelings and defends his behavior. "Poor girl! I knew I was offering her a great dishonor,—as runs the custom of her people,—but it was my only way out of a difficulty far more serious than it could have possibly appeared to her people."[36]

When writing about his fieldwork adventures, Cushing maintained an air of aloofness from the Zuni, although while living among them he often identified closely with them. Many of their beliefs he later called superstitions and survivals, but he also sided with them against the Navajo and the whites, actions which ultimately led to his being recalled to Washington. Not content merely to observe the behavior of the Zunis, he attempted to participate in their daily activities as much as he could. When, as a consequence of his persistence, he was forced to make concessions and to conform to the demands of his hosts, he often did so reluctantly, but also with respect and out of consideration for them. More than once he had to play the game of bluff to observe activities, to sketch, or to take notes. Some of his actions seem deceptive or unethical to us today, as perhaps they seemed to Cushing himself at the time. Yet he was as involved and sensitive as he was detached and determined. He ministered to the sick and dying; he interceded in the torture of a man accused of sorcery; he bestowed lavish attention upon his adopted father. When Cushing deceived the Zunis or shamed one of them, he often expressed self-dissatisfaction or felt remorse. When he was tricked or put on the defensive, he usually seemed to understand and appreciate the fact that turn about is fair play.

As instructed, Cushing "got the information." But his experiences while doing so, as recounted in "My Adventures in Zuñi," reveal the diverse and often unpredictable nature of events that occur when one engages in fieldwork. Cushing's adventures also demonstrate the ambivalent feelings that evolve as fieldworkers interact with the individuals whose behaviors constitute the subjects of their research.

We know about the reactions of Cushing and a few other fieldworkers to their research subjects. But for the most part, we know nothing about what subjects think of the individuals who observe and write about them. In the case of Cushing and other researchers who have done fieldwork among the Zuni, however, we are more fortunate. Some impressions and reactions of individual Zunis who encountered or were told about these fieldworkers have recently been documented and reported.

An elderly woman, born while Cushing was in Zuni, said that she had been named after Cushing's wife, Emma, a fact that suggests some affection or respect for the Cushings. "He was a good friend of the Indians and that's why he was made a Bow Priest," a ninety-year-old man remarked. In response to a question about Cushing, one Zuni woman stated, "Yes, my mother told me about Cushing. She told me that her folks were responsible for making him a Bow Priest. But just a few years after making him a Bow Priest three high priests were killed in the Ramah area and the people said that because those priests made that white man a high priest, they were killed.''[37] With this single exception, most published statements about Cushing are either positive or uncritical, perhaps because memory of him has faded or because Cushing had been well received generally.

The same cannot be said for Matilda Coxe Stevenson, whose husband, Colonel James Stevenson, had led the Smithsonian expedition of 1879, of which Cushing was a member. Mrs. Stevenson has been described by some contemporary researchers as "strong willed" and "overbearing." She is said to have reacted "much too aggressively" and to have lacked "a saving sense of humor.''[38] An elderly Zuni woman who knew Mrs. Stevenson said, "She was disliked by many Zunis. She lived in a camp which was guarded by two Zuni men whom she paid every day. Some of the Zunis wanted to get rid of her. You cannot believe how arrogant she was. She entered the *Kivas* without asking permission of the high priest. She took pictures because the Zunis did not know what she was doing.''[39] Her persistence in gaining admission to religious ceremonies and in obtaining sacred objects, however, earned her respect from at least some Zuni who admired her obvious fearlessness.[40] Others interviewed recently railed against Mrs. Stevenson, accusing her of having stolen sacred objects, a charge that seems to have had its origin in rumor rather than reality.[41] It has been suggested that Mrs. Stevenson had "a tendency to throw rapport to the winds" anyway, because of a sense of urgency in salvaging the old ways before they were irrevocably lost.[42] Zuni reaction to Mrs. Stevenson's book about their way of life was mixed at the time the work was first published in 1904. But some of the present-day Zunis reportedly have borrowed a copy surreptitiously from a local trader in order to study its pictures and descriptions of dancers.[43]

Elsie Clews Parsons, another fieldworker, was fondly remembered as "a real friend of my husband and me" by a Cherokee woman, married to a Zuni, who had been hostess to Mrs. Parsons. According to this woman, "We were her best friends and we worked hard for her. I am not a Zuni and I don't know everything about the Zunis. So if there was something which Mrs. Parsons wanted to know about them and I didn't know, I asked the people and they told me everything. My husband was an important Zuni and he helped her a lot.''[44]

Over the years, this Cherokee woman had also hosted such

well-known anthropologists as Leslie Spier, A. L. Kroeber, and Franz Boas. "When Mr. Kroeber was in Zuni for the first time," she recalled, "he came to see me and introduced himself by saying, 'My name is Alfred Kroeber. I am a friend of Mrs. Parsons. I am willing to eat beans three times a day. Will you accept me to live here for the summer?' I thought he was so cute that I agreed to rent him a room."[45]

Of another famous visitor the same woman remarked, "Professor Boas was a very pleasant person. He was not talkative like Mrs. Parsons; he was calm, quiet, and very sweet. He was a good cook. So long as he was with me, he was in charge of the kitchen and cooked dinner—mostly soup. Once he sent me a packet of all kinds of soup."[46]

More tarnished in the minds of some people is the image of another investigator. Archaeologist F. W. Hodge aroused considerable discomfort by excavating Hawikuh, one of the ancient settlements of the Zuni. By 1923 the Zunis were in the throes of religious factionalism. Hodge had wanted to make a film of some ceremonies. He had the approval of one faction, but not of the other. The opponents did more than merely protest. They smashed cameras and expelled both the photographer and Hodge from the pueblo.[47]

Ruth Benedict and Ruth Bunzel arrived on the scene a year later. Their immediate problem in the midst of community strife was to find a host family and a local sponsor. "When Nick Tumaka paid his official call on us that evening," writes Bunzel about their arrival, "to find out, as governor, who we were and what we were doing, we fished around for names that might identify us as acceptable. (The question was, 'Who sent you?') He didn't recognize Parsons, Kroeber, or Spier. When we mentioned Hodge, he bristled, and we took it right back. We didn't really know him well. Finally running out of names, we mentioned Boas. Boas had spent three days in Zuni when he was working at Laguna, but Nick remembered the man with the crooked face who had wanted to hear stories. That turned the trick and we got our visa."[48]

The interpreter for Bunzel and Benedict remembered them with mixed emotions. Of Bunzel she said, "She was just like a sister to me." Further, "Bunzel was a good woman. She liked people and was always good to children." There were some difficulties, however. "Once I got after her because she spoiled one of my nicest dresses. She borrowed it for a dance and then sat on the dirt floor wearing my dress. I remember her getting upset only once when she was followed by some boys who said dirty things to her. She talked back to them in Zuni and scolded them. They got scared and ran away." Bunzel apparently made several promises to her hostess which she did not fulfill, leaving the woman puzzled and disappointed. Of Benedict, the interpreter complained, "She did not go out, as Bunzel did. She would pick out someone and would bring him home and write down whatever he told her." This woman and others contended that Benedict's analysis could not have been well founded, lacking as she did an intimate knowledge of pueblo life. However, Benedict was, according to her interpreter, "more polite and generous than Bunzel. She spoke gently and gave more money." The remuneration, whatever its amount, was sufficient to enable the interpreter to purchase land. On it she built a house in which subsequent fieldworkers lived in a manner the woman conceived to be more fitting to their status.[49]

Not every fieldworker was invited to Zuni or permitted to stay, however. In 1941 the Tribal Council confiscated the notes of one researcher, burning part of them and demanding that the individual leave within twenty-four hours. Another investigator was threatened with expulsion, and several more have been denied facilities in Zuni for fieldwork.[50]

That the Zunis' experiences with past fieldworkers have created difficulties for contemporary investigators is exemplified by their reactions to Trikoli Nath Pandey, an American-trained anthropologist born in India. Pandey, whose research is the source of much of the available information about the Zunis' interactions with ethnologists, comments: "During the course of my fieldwork, many a time I was asked by the Zuni why I was studying them and not the whites. Once on meeting a white trader one of my informants said: 'Do you know any of these blood-sucking leeches? Believe me, they are really leeches. I guess you have people like them in India, too. Like the Navajos, they are everywhere.' "[51]

A middle-aged male Zuni complained to Pandey, "When we go to white men's places, we behave ourselves, but when they come to our pueblo they don't. They never let us do anything alone. They ask questions all the time."[52] Said another Zuni about fieldworkers, "They always sneak about and learn secrets

about people and write funny stories."⁵³ The governor objected,
"Nobody comes here to help us. Everyone who comes has his
own self-interest at heart."⁵⁴ And one man asked Pandey, "Are
we still so primitive that you anthropologists have to come to
study us every summer?"⁵⁵

The first host family with whom Pandey lived, and who
received one hundred dollars a month for keeping him, seemed
delighted to have a fieldworker for the summer. But reaction
was not unanimously positive. "Some members of the family
were always conscious that I was an anthropologist and believed
my only aim in being with them was 'to fish for secret information.' They did not enjoy answering my questions about their
culture and would ask me instead to tell them about the anthropologists whom they had known."⁵⁶ The same family accused
him of "selling Zuni secrets to white men."⁵⁷

Pandey stayed with another family the following summer. "I
soon discovered that the oldest woman of this family, the one
who had served as an interpreter to Benedict and Bunzel, was a
warmhearted person. She took a genuine interest in my work,
introduced me to her large number of kinsmen, and kept
encouraging me to learn the ways of her people. I believe," he
speculates, "her earlier contact with anthropologists was useful
to my work. She was appreciative for her contacts with outsiders and always asked me about the antropologists she had
helped earlier." When Pandey returned from visiting other
people, she would demand: "Tell us the news; you know more
about Zuni than anyone else here. When you go away, we certainly miss you."⁵⁸ Once when Pandey told her that Zuni
seemed to have changed a great deal over the years, her response
was, "So have anthropologists, You are not asking me what
Mr. Kroeber used to ask."⁵⁹

While drunk, the son-in-law of Pandey's hostess shouted at
him, "Bloody Hindu, come out. I know why you came here . . .
(name deleted) told me about you people (anthropologists). I
know you people are no good." But the family reprimanded
him, saying, "Don't treat him that way. He is an important person." Later, the son-in-law apologized for his behavior, but he
seemed resentful of the attention paid to Pandey.⁶⁰

"He is nice. We don't feel ashamed of him," Pandey's hostess told another person, referring to her anthropologist-guest.

"He is just like one of us. He eats with us and behaves good. We like him."[61]

To others, Pandey, having come from a remote land called India, was an object of curiosity and even of spiritual kinship. He was reminded that he was "a real Indian" and was even asked if perhaps his ancestors were also ancestors of the Zuni.

"I have been received differently by different people at Zuni," concludes Pandey. "The white people knew who I was and were invariably friendly and cooperative," although they were not the subjects of his research. "The Indians," whom he studied, "were rather ambivalent towards me as well as towards my work."[62]

The ambivalence Pandey describes is mutual. When people study people, all parties are necessarily ambiguous in their feelings toward each other—at least initially. Both fieldworkers and subjects of research must deal with dilemmas created by the nature of their relationship. Diverse problems arise in every fieldwork situation, and the individuals involved must make varied types of decisions. In citing at length Cushing's adventures among the Zunis, as well as the Zunis' reactions to Cushing and other fieldworkers, we hope to suggest the substance and scope of these dilemmas and to call attention to the fact that they are both rooted in, and resolved by, the shared human identity of the subjects.

The dichotomy between inquirer and subject is often drawn in the fieldwork literature. Yet what becomes readily apparent to those who engage in fieldwork is that the distinction is neither clear-cut nor consistent. Fieldworkers not only observe and question informants, but they are studied and queried themselves in a continual reversal of roles. Decisions made—sometimes with forethought, but often without prior consideration of the alternatives or consequences—reveal that sometimes one, and sometimes another, party to the act is in a position of dominance or control. "My Adventures in Zuñi" and other personal accounts of individuals' experiences as fieldworkers reveal the desirability, if not the inevitability, of an approach to fieldwork that focuses upon, rather than slights or ignores, the human element.

In the chapters that follow, we explore many of the issues that are discussed and debated in the scholarly literature on field-

work. Both published and unpublished accounts of fieldworkers' firsthand personal experiences are used to exemplify
these issues and to suggest how and why a pragmatic approach
to fieldwork might resolve the seeming dilemmas or better prepare one to generate and assess alternatives. We also raise a
number of questions that are seldom asked, and we propose
answers to them based upon our own experiences and those of
others who have learned, often by trial and error, that there are
many means to several ends, and that the means and ends are
interdependent, inseparable aspects of a complex of experiences
that define fieldwork and make it unique.

Alternative Means,
Many Ends

F ieldwork involving people studying people is an experience during which the participants learn by observing and querying each other at first hand. Parties to the act may be strangers, friends, or relatives, may be similar or different in physical appearance and social mores, and may be familiar or unfamiliar with the environments in which they encounter each other. The success of the endeavor, like that of any interaction, is dependent upon the willingness and ability of those involved to establish a meaningful basis for communicating.

Yet fieldwork is also a one-sided and a selfish act. Every fieldwork project has its inception in the mind of some individual who decides unilaterally that some other human being(s) will serve as the source or resource for information. Rarely are those who are considered and selected as subjects for fieldwork asked in advance if they are willing to be so identified; seldom are they requested to participate in the design of the fieldwork project or to judge and approve the plans that call for someone to observe and document their behavior.

Contrary to the impression given by authors of most field-based studies and research guides, fieldwork does not begin when investigator and informant first confront each other face to face. Rather, it commences when some individual decides (for whatever reason) that she or he will do fieldwork. To begin to comprehend the nature of fieldwork and to appreciate the role the human element plays in it, then, is to understand first the ways in which fieldwork projects evolve.

"When I sailed for Samoa," writes Margaret Mead, "I realized only very vaguely what a commitment to field work and writing about field work meant. My decision to become an anthropologist was based in part on my belief that a scientist, even one who had no great and special gift such as a great artist must have, could make a useful contribution to knowledge."[1] She continues, combining statements of general purpose with those indicative of personal motivation. "I had responded also to the sense or urgency that had been conveyed to me by Professor Boas and Ruth Benedict. Even in remote parts of the world ways of life about which nothing was known were vanishing before the onslaught of modern civilization. The work of recording these unknown ways of life had to be done now—*now* —or they would be lost forever. Other things could wait, but not this most urgent task."[2]

These justifications for doing fieldwork were supplemented further for Mead in the summer of 1924, when she attended a meeting of the British Association for the Advancement of Science in Toronto. All the anthropologists there, she admits, "talked about 'my people' and I had no people to talk about. From that time on I was determined to go to the field, not at some leisurely chosen later date, but immediately—as soon as I had completed the necessary preliminary steps."[3]

For Mead, the preliminaries included choosing a place (Polynesia) and a research topic (culture change), apparently in that order. Franz Boas was at first opposed to both. "He thought it was too dangerous" for her to go abroad, Mead reports, "and recited a sort of litany of young men who had died or been killed while working outside the United States. He wanted me to work among American Indians."[4] Since Boas's approval was essential if Mead were to receive the fellowship necessary to enable her to do fieldwork, she was "willing to compromise and study the adolescent girl,"[5] though not to abandon her plans to work in Polynesia, about which she had some vicarious knowledge since Polynesian cultures had been the subject of her doctoral dissertation. Boas finally agreed. He refused to permit Mead to go to the Tuamotu Islands as she had originally proposed, however, for they were too remote. He insisted that she select instead an island served regularly by ship. Mead chose

Samoa because, "among all the less spoiled Polynesian islands, a steamer went there every three weeks."[6]

In Mead's case, place took precedence over everything else. The specific people and topic for investigation were negotiable, but locale was not. For Peggy Golde, however, choices of field site and research subjects grew out of a general interest in a particular phenomenon and were determined by a single, and seemingly inconsequential, act.

"Seated sidesaddle," writes Golde, "I had to cling to the saddle horn for balance as the mule lurched up the narrow rocky path scratched into the mountainside. I could look across the deep valley at distant purple graphs of mountains outlined against the uniform blue of the sky while idly wondering, 'What am I doing here?' "[7] The reason she was on her way to an isolated Mexican Indian village, Golde reports, "was both the end and the beginning of a detective story that had begun with my interest in doing a study of art in its cultural context and with the purchase of a painted pot, on a previous trip to Mexico in 1956, from the museum of popular art in Mexico City...."[8] Golde continues, explaining the pertinence of her purchase to the fieldwork project she planned and conducted. "The painted decoration, set off in cartoonlike panels bordered by geometric and floral forms, depicted a menacing leonine animal ready to pounce on a bird, and a horse trampling a man wearing spurs. Notably distinctive both in style and content in comparison to the simple repetitive pottery painting I had seen in Chiapas, Oaxaca, and Michoacan, this work so engaged me that I decided on the spot that I would someday locate the village where it had been made and do my fieldwork there."[9] She "could make such a decision," Golde notes, "because the problem I wanted to study was the nature of the development of art style, the meaning of both symbolic and formal features characteristic of the style, and the relation between style and aesthetic values."[10]

Having determined what she would like to study and where she could do so raised questions as to how Golde would proceed. "Since relatively little attention had been paid by anthropologists to problems in the study of art and culture," she asserts, "I had no clear idea what aspects of the culture might be relevant to focus on; I knew how to study style itself, but I had no hypotheses about what style might be expressing."[11] Yet while she could not hypothesize about the phenomena the visual scene represented, Golde assumed that it must reflect other cultural phenomena and be rooted in culturally-based and shared emotions. "The hostility depicted in the pottery decoration," she writes, "pointed to a way to begin—to search for the sources of anger and aggression in the culture and the mode of its expression in other behaviors."[12]

With the help of the museum director, Golde located the village in which the pot she purchased had been made. During the fourteen months she spent there, she learned about "witchcraft beliefs, sex roles and relations between the sexes, attitudes toward illness and health, the conception of work, the suppression of anger, and the pervasive insecurity that characterized the people's outlook on the world," all of which, Golde states, "had shaped their aesthetic values and were embedded in the style."[13]

Unlike Mead and Golde, who had no firsthand knowledge of their research populations before they assumed the fieldworker's role, sociologist Seymour Martin Lipset was acquainted with the individuals who would serve as subjects for one of his fieldwork projects long before he had generated a topic for investigation. From the time he was a child, Lipset had been witness to the activities of members of the International Typographical Union. "My father was a lifelong member of the union," Lipset writes. "He had been a printer in tsarist Russia before he emigrated to the United States and had belonged to the printers union there."[14] Lipset continues, indicating the impact of these circumstances on him, "While in elementary school and high school, I frequently overheard discussions of union matters, and occasionally my father would take me to the monthly meetings of the New York local, which were held on Sunday afternoons at Stuyvesant High School—a set of experiences which was to play a role later in my conceiving of the 'occupational community' as an important part of the environment of the union."[15]

It was while he was a high school and beginning college student in the late 1930s and early 1940s, Lipset reports, that his interest in union politics began to evolve. He belonged to the Young People's Socialist League and became involved in socialist causes. As he and others learned about the stormy events that were occurring in Europe during that era—"Stalin's bloody purges and show trials," the destruction of "anti-Communist socialists and anarchists" in Franco's Spain, and the "triumph of Nazism in Germany," for example[16]—it seemed that the trade-union movement was "incapable of offering the type of effective leadership which might make significant social reform possible."[17] Instead, it became clear that "most movements which were dedicated to social reform, a reduction in class exploitation, and an increase in democracy did not act to further these objectives once they held any significant share of power."[18] Yet while this was generally true, Lipset notes, the International Typographical Union seemed to be an exception. "Here was a large trade-union which governed itself through an elaborate democratic political system. Members frequently defeated leadership politics in referendums. Perhaps of even greater significance," Lipset adds, "was the turnover of union officers on a national and local level. International officers as well as the heads of large locals were defeated for re-election in contests conducted under rules that protected the rights of opposition and willingly gave up office to return to work in the print shop—phenomena which occurred rarely, if ever, in other trade-unions."[19] To Lipset, it was important to determine why this was so. When time and opportunity made it possible, he designed and implemented a fieldwork project through which the hypotheses he had evolved could be tested.[20]

The desire to work in a particular locale, to study the makers of a certain material object, and to solve a specific problem served as stimuli for fieldwork projects designed and carried out by Mead, Golde, and Lipset, respectively. By contrast, James West began with a research topic and a set of criteria that could guide him in the selection of a place and population. Yet despite West's prior planning, the site in which he worked and the people who became the subjects for his investigation were determined more by accident than by design.

West's wish was "to learn specifically and in detail how one relatively isolated and still 'backward' American farming community reacts to the constant stream of traits and influences pouring into it from cities and from the more 'modern' farming communities."[21] Writes West, "For reasons unnecessary to relate, the selection was limited to the general region of the southern Midwest. Within this area the search was for a town with not over 1,000 inhabitants, which was still a lively trading and social center for farmers living within its trade area. To simplify my research task," West continues, "I sought a community which had the fewest possible economic and social factors which might complicate the problem under scrutiny. This means, economically, that no town was considered if its inhabitants drew any important portion of their income from mines, factories, summer resorts, or any other industrial or urbanizing activity that would confuse the economics of a traditional farming community."[22] Furthermore, "It means, socially, that the presence of any foreign-language-speaking group in or near a town, or of Negroes, or of any large non-Protestant or 'atypical' religious congregation eliminated the town from consideration."[23] Finally, he adds, "A further requirement was that the community should be as 'level' as possible socially and economically. It should have no recognized 'aristocracy' or other well-defined social 'classes,' and I hoped to find a community where people were all living as nearly as possible on the same social and financial plane."[24]

West visited thirty towns, rejecting each for unstated reasons. "Most frequently, however," he asserts, "the eliminating factor was a *highway*."[25] But the town he did select "was discovered by accident. On a flinty detour through Woodland County my car broke down. Repairs at the Ford garage in Plainville took two days, and these days convinced me that Plainville was the town I had been looking for."[26] So West studied the people of Plainville and made them the subject of a book, despite the fact that the town was smaller than he wished, more socially and economically stratified than he suspected, and close to the construction site of a new transcontinental highway.[27]

Like James West, Adrian C. Mayer chose his topic before selecting a specific place or population. "My intended focus of research was the caste system," he writes. "I wanted to know what was involved in being a member of a caste society, what the caste system actually meant 'on the ground.'"[28] Mayer, too, established a set of criteria for choosing site and people that grew out of the topic in which he was interested. "My research aim," Mayer notes, "led me to seek a village with a good complement of castes; I also wanted it to be one which was being affected by changes brought about since the merger of the princely state it had formed part of, and which was thus in contact with towns, though beyond the orbit of urban commuting."[29] Some administrators in Indore, the state capital of

India's Dewas district, suggested that area for Mayer's consideration. After exploring "half a dozen places" within the district "that fitted my criteria," Mayer states, he chose Ramkheri. It "had a fairly full complement of functional castes; it had been included in a newly-opened community development block, yet was not a village sending commuters to Dewas or Indore; it had had ties with the Maharaja, yet was now part of the new state; and it could provide me with accommodation."[30]

That the nature, as well as the availability, of accommodation was a decisive factor in Mayer's choice of Ramkheri is made clear as he continues. "This last was a most important consideration. In other places, I had been offered part of a house, or a cattle byre in a compound. But I knew from previous fieldwork that such accommodation had drawbacks: one tended to be identified with a single family, and one's freedom of movement might be restricted."[31] The house offered to Mayer was outside the village. "But I saw in this a possible advantage for the sort of study I hoped to conduct, in a society which I expected to be so clearly stratified," he asserts. "To live on neutral ground would, I hoped, make it easier for me to see people of both high and low castes since I would not be linked to a high or low caste ward or street."[32] Mayer felt that there could also be additional advantages to living in the house, for it "stood near the metalled road; its well was a place where travellers stopped to refresh themselves and their bullocks, and it had become the villagers' waiting place for the handful of buses which ran along the road each day."[33]

Once Mayer was settled in the house in Ramkheri, he had, as he had hoped, numerous visitors, "My verandah usually had people sitting on it, smoking, drinking tea and gossiping," he writes. "But my hope of entertaining an even spread of castes was not fulfilled. In part this was because the lower castes went less often to town by bus, and thus did not wait for transportation near the house; in part it was more generally because I was caught up in the village's caste situation, and would have been wherever I had lived. It was impossible for me merely to 'observe' the caste system," Mayer notes; "I had to participate in it, by the fact of my living in Ramkheri."[34] Thus, while the availability of a house on what he felt would be neutral ground was a major factor in his choice of a fieldwork site, Mayer "could not avoid being 'placed' in the commensal hierarchy, with all the implications that this entailed.''[35] The people identified him ''as a person of undesignated upper caste status''[36]; and the extent and nature of his access to, and relationships with, the villagers were determined by this ascribed identity, not by the location of his place of residence.

Both West and Mayer established sets of criteria before selecting places in which to conduct the kinds of fieldwork projects they wished to undertake. Neither researcher reveals the reasons or bases for establishing such criteria or explains how his research topic evolved. For both, however, practical considerations played a decisive part in the selection of field sites. West may or may not have discovered and studied Plainville if his automobile had not broken down there; Mayer might or might not have chosen to work in Ramkheri if the only accommodations had been in the homes of villagers identified with specific castes. The fact that unexpected car trouble and the opportunity to live in a house on the periphery of a village influenced West's and Mayer's choices of locales suggests the pragmatic, arbitrary, and human nature of the decisions fieldworkers make.

That personal and practical concerns can sometimes take precedence and serve as the principal determinants of fieldwork topic, site, and population is illustrated by the experiences of Leela Dube. She writes: ''Anthropology for me is a happy by-product of marriage. In 1954, I married S. C. Dube who was then working for his Ph.D. in social anthropology. A few months after our wedding, I accompanied him on his second field trip among the Kamar, a tribe of shifting cultivators living in central India.''[37] Dube suggests that she had no difficulties adjusting to life in the field. ''My husband had stayed in most of these villages on his earlier visits and had established close contacts with the people, who received him and me with much warmth,'' she states. ''I was not treated as a stranger and did not have to make any special effort to seek acceptance from the Kamar. I was welcome as the wife of a friendly outsider who had endeared himself to the people.''[38]

During this sojourn among the Kamar, Dube quickly came to realize ''that anthropology was to be an integral part of the content of my marriage.''[39] She watched her husband work and assisted him by obtaining ''from Kamar women some information on essentially feminine matters.''[40] Uneasy at first and tempted to back out, Dube persisted, for this ''was the crucial period of my adjustment with my husband. There was also a kind of challenge in the work," she asserts, "for my idealistic impulse to get close to the common people and to understand them was being realized."[41]

Upon the couple's return to Nagpur, Dube completed requirements for the master's degree in political science. Then she began planning her work for the doctorate in anthropology, which apparently entailed her generating and carrying out a fieldwork project on her own. She explains how and why she evolved the plans for the project she was to undertake.

"Both my husband and my father-in-law suggested that I should work among the Gond who lived in the southern part of Chhattisgarh," reports Dube. "My being a woman was what lay behind this advice. Unlike the Kamar and the Bhunjia (the latter were my husband's choice for his second field study), the Gond were settled agriculturists and lived in relatively accessible villages."[42] She continues, indicating other advantages of working among the Gond. "Their language of communication, within and outside the tribe, was Chhattisgarhi which I had already learned. My father-in-law, who had then taken charge of the area in the capacity of a civil servant (manager, Court of Wards), assured me that if I worked among the Gond of Bindranawagarh zamindari he would be able to take care of me."[43] She explains what this would entail. "He promised to provide me with a bullock-cart and a reliable driver, and to arrange for various kinds of help and care."[44] Having heard the tale of a woman sociologist who had failed in her efforts to collect folklore in Chhattisgarh "because of the behaviour of petty officials and the ununderstanding and indifferent attitude of the people,"[45] Dube decided to do her fieldwork among the Gond and "under the protective umbrella"[46] of her father-in-law.

Dube studied the Gond between 1947 and 1950, making "several visits to the area, altogether spending ten months in the field."[47] She describes her experiences, elaborating further on the ways in which her father-in-law aided her. "As a well-protected daughter-in-law I travelled the Gond country in a bullock-cart accompanied by a maid-servant and escorted by a peon. The maid-servant, who had been specially engaged to be with me in the field, belonged to the caste of cattle herders and water carriers. She cooked for me and acted as a personal attendant."[48] Dube discusses another important function that the maid fulfilled. "It was she who answered the inevitable queries about me: that I was the wife of the only son of the manager, that my mother-in-law had died in my husband's childhood, and that I was writing a book on Gond women, and so on."[49] The data Dube gathered during her field trips to Chhattisgarh served as the basis for her doctoral dissertation (unpublished), *The Gond Woman* (Nagpur University, 1956).

"Very few Indian women have undertaken anthropological fieldwork in remote tribal areas," writes Dube, in conclusion. "I consider myself fortunate in this respect. I was in a particularly happy situation. I was married, enjoyed a status, and there were satisfactory arrangements for my movement and stay. All this was necessary for being able to do fieldwork among the Gond."[50]

For Helen Codere, as for Leela Dube, personal and practical considerations played the determining part in the generation of a fieldwork project. The specifics differed, however, and the decisions made were apparently Codere's alone. "My choice of area, East Central Africa, and culture, Rwanda, was in general the belated choice of the kind of place I wanted for my field work when I first joined anthropology in part, at least, to see the world," Codere writes.[51] It was a belated choice, she explains, because World War II was in progress when she was ready to begin fieldwork, making it impossible for American anthropologists to work outside the New World. So Codere chose as her research population the Kwakiutl Indians of Vancouver Island, British Columbia. By the end of the war, however, Codere found that the Kwakiutl "were neither numerous nor different enough to satisfy the earlier personal and scientific craving to live and work in a large, relatively unacculturated, and, to me, exotic population."[52] So she looked to Africa as an appropriate place in which to study change.

"Narrowing the choice to an area of Africa in which English was not the mediating language again involved a mixture of personal and scientific reasons," Codere asserts. "Some of these were, if not impeccable, at least objective and arguable, such as the desire to work where the anthropological tradition had not been set up by British social anthropology, much of which seems to produce beautiful entomological accounts of various human hives. I also needed to go somewhere where basic ethnography had been done over time, so that something might be accomplished in a period limited to one year.''[53]

Codere follows these statements of professional preference and practical necessity with those indicative of additional personal motivations. ''Some of my reasons, if not disreputable, were highly subjective. My first confession along these lines is that I thought I would function best where it was not too hot much of the time. Rwanda, though near the equator, had an elevation that guaranteed a temperate climate, which did favor work.''[54] She continues: ''My next confession is of a sort I suspect many anthropologists might make, although I have known only one to admit, as I shall do, that place and tribal names have an irresistible appeal. In my case,'' Codere explains, ''they have had since I first heard of 'Timbuctoo' or of the 'Onandaga' or the other five tribes of the Iroquois League. On this score, 'Rwanda or Ruanda' could hardly miss, with its twin kingdom of 'Urundi' (now 'Burundi' which is just as good), its access via 'Usumbura,' its capital of 'Nyanza,' and its populace divided among the 'Tutsi' ('Batutsi'), 'Hutu' ('Bahutu'), and 'Twa' ('Batwa') castes. For a nomenclature gourmet, these were but staples in a feast of names, every one of which was a delight.''[55] Onomastic appeal, Codere notes, ''is a less trivial basis of attraction to an area and culture than might be supposed, when the addition of marvelous new names can be an almost daily pleasure. After all,'' she adds, almost as an afterthought, ''pleasures of any kind can be rather meagerly laid on in the field, and one that can contribute to learning personal and place names and the language, offers no major distractions, and produces no hangovers is not to be despised.''[56]

Codere's remarks illustrate the varied and unpredictable human factors that can affect the decisions made as individuals conceptualize fieldwork projects. She not only exemplifies the role that personal motives play in the decision-making process, but she also defends those that figured prominently in her choices of field site and research population, explaining why she considers them neither irrelevant nor unimportant. Codere's stance is indicative of a growing tendency among fieldworkers to recognize and reveal, rather than to deny or conceal, the part that personal interests, preferences, and experiences play in the formulation of fieldwork plans.

That fieldwork projects are often engendered and shaped by deeply-rooted human curiosities, needs, and biases is merely suggested by Codere. Other individuals demonstrate more explicitly the close correlations between their personal histories and the kinds of plans they formulate for fieldwork. One such person is William Foote Whyte.

"I come from a very consistent upper-middle-class background,"[57] writes Whyte in an essay appended to his widely-read book *Street Corner Society: The Social Structure of an Italian Slum* (Chicago, 1943) and published as part of the second edition of that work (1955). He elaborates: "One grandfather was a doctor; the other, a superintendent of schools. My father was a college professor. My upbringing, therefore, was very far removed from the life I have described in Cornerville."[58]

While a student at Swarthmore College, Whyte notes, his principal interests were in economics and writing. Some of his short stories were published in the campus literary magazine, and three of his one-act plays were produced in conjunction with a playwriting competition at the college. His aspirations for a writing career were called into question, he admits, when he tried to generate a novel. "Even as I wrote the concluding chapters," Whyte asserts, "I realized that the manuscript was worthless. I finished it, I suppose, just so that I could say to myself that I had written a novel."[59] Yet he did not feel that the experience was without benefit. "This writing was valuable to me," notes Whyte, "largely in what it taught me about myself."[60]

Whyte explains what he learned from his unsuccessful writing attempt. "Now I had read the often-given advice to young writers that they should write out of their own experience, so I had no reason to be ashamed of this limitation. On the other hand, it was when I reflected upon my experience that I became uneasy and dissatisfied."[61] Whyte elaborates: "My home life had been very happy and intellectually stimulating—but without adventure. I had never had to struggle over anything. I knew lots of nice people, but almost all of them came from good, solid middle-class backgrounds like my own.... I knew nothing about the slums (or the gold coast for that matter). I knew nothing about life in the factories, fields, or mines—

except what I had gotten out of books. So I came to feel that I was a pretty dull fellow."[62]

His "interest in economics and social reform also led in the direction of *Street Corner Society,*"[63] Whyte notes as he describes further the personal factors that contributed to the evolution of his fieldwork project. "One of my most vivid college memories is of a day spent with a group of students in visiting the slums of Philadelphia. I remember it not only for the image of dilapidated buildings and crowded people but also for the sense of embarrassment I felt as a tourist in the district. I had the common young man's urge to do good to these people, and yet I knew then that the situation was so far beyond anything I could realistically attempt at the time that I felt like an insincere dabbler even to be there."[64] Yet despite his initial uneasiness, Whyte "began to think sometimes about going back to such a district and really learning to know the people and the conditions of their lives."[65]

The opportunity to do so came when Whyte graduated from Swarthmore in 1936 and was offered a three-year research fellowship by the Society of Fellows at Harvard University. "The only restriction," he states, "was that I was not allowed to accumulate credits toward a Ph.D. degree,"[66] a stipulation that he subsequently came to regard as advantageous. "If I had been allowed to work for the Ph.D.," writes Whyte, "I suppose I should have felt that I must take advantage of the time and the opportunity. With this avenue cut off, I was forced to do what I wanted to do, regardless of academic credits."[67]

In continuing to trace the evolution of his field research, Whyte demonstrates the correlations between his earlier experiences and the decisions he made. "I began with a vague idea that I wanted to study a slum district. Eastern City provided several possible choices. In the early weeks of my Harvard fellowship I spent some of my time talking [sic] up and down the streets of the various slum districts of Eastern City and talking with people in social agencies about these districts."[68] His choice of a locale in which to work, Whyte admits, was made "on very unscientific grounds: Cornerville best fitted my picture of what a slum district should look like. Somehow I had developed a picture of run-down three- to five-story buildings crowded in together. The dilapidated wooden-frame buildings of some other parts of the city did not look quite genuine to me."[69] Whyte qualifies these assertions to indicate that his decision was not totally arbitrary or idiosyncratic. "To be sure, Cornerville did have one characteristic that recommended it on a little more objective basis. It had more people per acre living in it than any other section of the city. If a slum meant overcrowding, this was certainly it."[70]

Having found his slum district, Whyte began to contemplate his work. His initial plan—to carry out a community study requiring the services of ten researchers—evoked unfavorable reactions from the secretary of Harvard's Society of Fellows, who found the proposed project too ambitious and unrealistic. Stunned at first by this unexpected response, Whyte eventually came to realize the defensibility of the criticisms and set about revising his project design. He consulted with Harvard professors, friends, and community members; read extensively in the fields of sociology and anthropology; and enrolled in several courses at Harvard that familiarized him with relevant scholarly literature and provided him with experiences in conducting surveys and interviews. During the three and a half years he devoted to his fieldwork project, Whyte often found it necessary to revise his research goals and procedures. Yet he maintained as his focal point a locale and people that had first been suggested by a visit to a Philadelphia slum neighborhood and by his self-awareness of the desirability of extending his horizons beyond those provided by his upper-middle-class background, training, and associations.

Like Whyte, Hortense Powdermaker conceived and carried out a fieldwork project that had its roots in memorable personal experiences. It evolved after completion of her first field venture in the village of Lesu on the island of New Ireland in the Mandated Territory of New Guinea (1929-1930). Upon returning to the United States, Powdermaker was awarded a National Research Council fellowship that afforded her the time needed to prepare her Lesu field data for publication. Once the volume was completed,[71] she wondered what would be in store for her. Edward Sapir, chairman of the anthropology department at Yale University, where Powdermaker had a research position with the Institute of Human Relations, suggested two possible research populations: a North American Indian tribe and a Hassidic Jewish group in New York City. "Because of my British training," writes Powdermaker, "I knew little about American Indians, and furthermore, was not interested in them."[72] Her reaction to Sapir's second suggestion was also negative because of "lack of interest, no knowledge of Hebrew or Yiddish, and a feeling that I lacked the necessary objectivity to study Orthodox Jews."[73] When Sapir asked her whom she would like to study, Powdermaker promptly replied, "American Negroes." Sapir responded: "Fine. Draw up a project and submit it to the Social Science Research Council."[74]

Powdermaker relates what happened next. "I went back to my office, and, to my surprise, within a few hours I had made a detailed plan to study a community in the deep South. I must have been thinking, consciously and unconsciously, for a long time about this type of research problem."[75] Growing up in Baltimore, she reports, had made her "aware of Negroes."[76] Her family employed female Negro daytime servants, and she had been particularly fond of a Negro seamstress who came regularly to her parents' home to sew and make clothes for the Powdermakers. In walking through Baltimore neighborhoods populated by blacks, she had noticed children peering from windows and families assembled outdoors on the steps during the warm summer months.

"One incident relating to Negroes stands out vividly from my years at home," Powdermaker continues. "I was coming home on a streetcar late one hot August afternoon from the playground where I taught during some summer vacations while a college student. White and Negro men who had obviously been digging and working in the sun boarded the car. They were all dirty and sweaty."[77] She elaborates further, explaining why the incident was memorable. "The car was crowded and people had to stand close to each other. A white woman standing by me complained about the smell of the Negroes; they did smell. I wondered about the white workers and moved next to them; they smelled, too. The blue cotton uniform which I wore as a playground teacher was wet with perspiration from my strenuous day. I then became aware that I smelled. The streetcar incident stood out as a discovery."[78]

Powdermaker notes that she had no Negro friends while growing up. The schools she attended were all white. The situation did not change when she entered Goucher College; as far as she knew, no black students were enrolled in that institution during her undergraduate days there. "The first Negro I met socially," writes Powdermaker, "was a woman student at the University of London when I was studying there. She was reading at the British Museum, where I spent much of my time. A mutual friend introduced us and we all went to tea at the usual four o'clock break."[79] Powdermaker describes her reaction to her new acquaintance: "I was enormously curious about this young Negro woman, but also exceedingly self-conscious. She knew I came from Baltimore, and I felt myself being watched. We became friends, although never close. Actually," she continues, "we did not have too much in common; but my curiosity (and probably hers too) promoted a friendly casual relationship for a couple of years. I learned that she was not much different from anyone else I knew. Her experiences as a Negro seemed only to give her personality a certain slant."[80]

The project Powdermaker devised to solicit financial support to do fieldwork among American Negroes pleased Edward Sapir, and he recommended its approval. But the choice of a site remained. "I had never been in the South," Powdermaker notes, "and my knowledge of it was casual. After considerable reading and thinking, I tentatively chose Mississippi; it seemed to represent the deep South, and no social studies had yet been done there. I left the selection of the exact community until I knew more about the local situation."[81]

Her request for aid approved, Powdermaker departed for the South in September of 1932. She went first to Fisk University, where she consulted with Charles S. Johnson and Franklin E. Frazier, blacks with reputations as distinguished scholars and as recognized experts on their own people. "They agreed that Mississippi was a good choice for a study," Powdermaker notes, "but said that I could not go there, 'pitch my tent,' and say, 'I've come to study you,' as I had done in Lesu. They thought I should enter the community through some easily understandable role in the state's education department."[82] Realizing the probable wisdom of such a suggestion, Powdermaker concurred. After several weeks on the Fisk University campus, during which time she socialized with blacks and was sometimes identified as one of them, she traveled to Oxford, Mississippi, where she consulted with a sociology professor at the state university. He was a cousin of the state superintendent of education and gave Powdermaker a letter of introduction to the man, with whom she discussed her plans when she arrived in Jackson. He, too, provided a letter, this time to state education officials, in which he requested that they assist Powdermaker in her research.

"My main problem at this point," notes Powdermaker, "was the choice of locale. I desired a county in which the old single-crop cotton plantation system still functioned, along with recent developments such as the New Deal program for diversification of crops."[83] She elaborates further. "My premise was that new economic patterns would probably influence social life and attitudes; I wanted to study the past and the contemporary. It amused me to see how quickly my early historical interests asserted themselves. A further condition for choosing a site would be the presence of county election officials, white and Negro, on whose cooperation I might count."[84]

With the assistance of a representative from the Rockefeller Foundation for Negro education in Jackson, Powdermaker narrowed her choice to three Mississippi counties. After being introduced to those charged with the improvement of Negro education in those areas during a statewide meeting she attended with the Rockefeller Foundation representative, Powdermaker made her decision. She explains how and why. "One of the three supervisors, Mrs. Wilson from Sunflower County, seemed decidedly superior. Her participation in the discussion was intelligent and vigorous. Mr. Green introduced me to her after the meeting was over. We liked each other immediately; I felt there would be no problem in working with her and she was eager to have me come to Indianola, the seat of Sunflower County, where she lived."[85] An additional factor contributed to the selection. "Mr. Green told me that Mr. Smith, the white superintendent of education in that county, was moderately liberal by Mississippi standards. He had been to a northern university for a year on a Rosenwald fellowship, while most of the other superintendents had never been outside of Mississippi. So, it was settled. I would live and work in Indianola and the surrounding rural area, part of the delta region formed by the Yazoo and Mississippi rivers."[86]

That her motivation for conducting fieldwork in a Mississippi community was deeply rooted in past experiences and ongoing concerns seemed apparent to Powdermaker from the start. It was some time later, however, that she discovered the nature of the correlations. "Many years after my Mississippi study," she writes, "I learned during a period of psychoanalysis that my interest in Negroes was no accident. However, the desire to go south and study the Negroes (and the whites there) sprang not only from deep and unconscious interests, but also from an intuitive return to my involvement with society."[87]

This "involvement with society" is discussed at length in the autobiographical preface to her book *Stranger and Friend: The Way of an Anthropologist* (New York, 1966). During her college days at Goucher, she explains, she had "developed socialistic interests, shared by only a few fellow students. For several weeks" she writes, "three of us debated with great seriousness whether it was right to accept inherited wealth. I took the negative position." She continues: "I 'discovered' the Baltimore slums and the trade-union movement. My belief in the latter was naive, simple, and ardent: poverty could be eradicated and the world would be better, if all workers joined unions. I had little concern with Marxian theory, or the political party. My interest in the labor movement was in part an expression of rebellion from the family, which made it no less socially legitimate."[88]

Motivated by these concerns, Powdermaker "began to explore the world of the workers, and spent a spring vacation working in a small unorganized men's shirt factory."[89] She "helped to revive the local Women's Trade Union League and became its representative to the Baltimore Federation of Labor...."[90] Furthermore, she became acquainted with "the local officers and some members of the International Ladies' Garment Workers' Union and the Amalgamated Clothing Workers of America...."[91] After graduating from college, she obtained an office job in the New York headquarters of the latter organization and eventually became one of its labor organizers. "Active participation in the lives of factory workers," she states, "helped me understand a segment of the American class system to which I did not belong—what it was not, as well as what it was. A social movement became a complex living force rather than an abstraction."[92]

In her role as union organizer, Powdermaker traveled to several eastern cities, making speeches, rallying workers, and negotiating with management personnel. Despite her success at this endeavor, Powdermaker's initial enthusiasm for the labor-union movement began to ebb. The difficulties involved in organizing workers, the power struggles within the unions themselves, and the uncertainty about the kind of life she would lead if she remained committed to union causes led her to resign her position.

Following her resignation, Powdermaker went to England— "partly," she asserts, "because I wanted to go there and partly to put an ocean between me and many personal ties in the labor movement."[93] After settling in London, she enrolled in two courses at the University of London in the fall of 1925. She dropped geology, which she found boring. The other course, social anthropology, fascinated her. It was taught by Bronislaw Malinowski. "The anthropology course opened new doors," notes Powdermaker. "I had found a discipline which, more than any other I knew, provided an understanding of man and his society, about which I was so curious."[94] Though she had no aspirations to work toward an advanced degree, Powdermaker eventually became a doctoral student in anthropology because of Malinowski's influence. Her Lesu fieldwork, carried out after she had earned the Ph.D., she deemed lacking in the involvement with society that had motivated and characterized her labor-union activities. After she returned to the United States, however, her involvement with society resurfaced. "When I left the labor movement," remarks Powdermaker, "I had naively thought that I should and could separate my concern about society from research. But, as James Coleman has noted, research can be rooted in a deep concern with society."[95] Her study of Mississippi Negroes, the second fieldwork project she undertook, had its roots in social concerns and personal experiences that were themselves intricately intertwined and obviously inseparable.

The foregoing characterizations of the evolution of fieldwork projects—presented largely in the words of the individuals who have described their experiences in print—demonstrate why insight into fieldwork must begin with an understanding of how plans for fieldwork unfold. The widely-held assumption that there is *a* way or a *correct* way to do fieldwork is immediately called into question when the planning procedures employed by experienced fieldworkers are considered and compared. As the accounts described and discussed above clearly illustrate, there is no common starting point for the fieldwork-planning process.

Individuals may begin by selecting a research topic, a locale, or some particular human being(s) whom they wish to make the subject(s) of their investigations. Their selections may be governed by specific criteria or determined by circumstance; even in the former case, unexpected occurrences and opportunities may require, or result in, the modification, supplementation, or complete abandonment of criteria deemed necessary or desirable in generating fieldwork projects.

Also apparent from fieldworkers' characterizations of the inception and formulation of their research plans is the fact that they, like those whom they choose to study, are first and foremost human beings. Hence, human and personal factors begin to play a prominent part in fieldwork from the moment individuals decide to engage in that activity. Statements of purpose and lists of objectives often suggest that fieldworkers are detached and impartial observers, documenters, analysts, and reporters whose ''scientific'' aims enable them to transcend their humanity and conduct their research unencumbered by presuppositions, assumptions, conceptions, expectations, personal motives, feelings, or biases. But inquiry does not—indeed *cannot*—occur in vacuo: every human being presupposes and assumes, comprehends reality in terms of learned concepts and relationships, and continuously categorizes and catalogues phenomena intellectually. Furthermore, engaging in fieldwork is a purposeful act, and fieldworkers are always motivated to assume that role for personal, pragmatic, and human reasons: to fulfill requirements for a course or academic degree, to earn the right to be identified professionally in a particular way, to gain recognition or remuneration, to satisfy a longing for discovery or adventure, to resolve or escape some personal crisis, or to understand self more completely by knowing others better. Recognizing the role that human factors play in the planning of fieldwork prepares one to realize and appreciate the importance and complexity of such factors when fieldworkers and informants first encounter each other face to face and are confronted with the task of establishing a mutually-understandable and acceptable basis for communicating.

Confrontation

Prophetically, my collecting of slave reminiscences began in an old house on a cold and dreary Halloween night in Bloomington, Indiana," writes Gladys Fry in the preface to her book *Night Riders in Black Folk History* (Knoxville, 1975). "As a graduate student beginning the research for my dissertation," she continues, "I had an uneasy feeling about the venture which the long walk from Indiana University's campus had not helped to erase." Fry enumerates her concerns. "I felt I should do more library research; I had qualms about the number of people I had invited to my first group session; I wondered if my ancient tape recorder would hold up." But her worry about practical matters, she makes clear, was only one cause of her uneasiness. "Leaving the security of the library carrel," she notes, "was like cutting an academic umbilical cord. Here I was in the field—ready or not. My disquietude was not helped by the fact that it was dark and rainy and I was alone—and the house where my informants waited faced a cemetery."[1]

Arriving at her destination, she encountered seven people who also had to meet *her*. And Gladys-Marie Fry, fieldworker, faced herself. As she had feared, things did not go smoothly at first. "At ten o'clock," she writes, "I was aware of the chimes from the University library tower. The interviews which had begun three hours earlier had not gone well." She explains why. "My questionnaire was unwieldy. I had too many questions and it took too much time to repeat the same questions and listen to the replies of each informant." Fry elaborates: "The real problem lay in these replies, which were evasive, avoiding any relevant discussion of the slave system. In fact, three of the informants were anxious to disassociate themselves from any connection with slavery. All wanted to discuss the Black question today, exhibiting bitterness about their plight as Blacks." In continuing, Fry reveals her expectations and characterizes what actually occurred. "A full evening had already passed and all I had heard were superficial reminiscences about slavery 'times,' but no extended accounts about specific events or occurrences. I suddenly realized I had struck a solid wall of resistance. But why? I knew the slave experience is very much a part of Black oral tradition, so why wouldn't they talk to me—really talk, not just politely parry questions?"[2]

An unanticipated incident proved auspicious. "Suddenly there was a loud crackling noise that seemed to come from the unoccupied upstairs," Fry reports. "We all looked around and at each other. Then everybody smiled. 'This old house is settling,' somebody offered by way of explanation." Fry capitalized on the remark. " 'Well,' I said, secretly relieved to shift the direction of the questioning, 'this gives me a chance to ask if anybody knows any ghost stories?' Mrs. Smith, a short, pinch-faced woman who had previously said little, replied promptly with great feeling. 'Don't you know the white man taught them all of that about ghosts. That was a way of keeping them down—keeping them under control.' " Fry characterizes what followed: "Then she described her grandmother's account of the overseer riding through the slave quarters covered with a white sheet, tin cans tied to his horse's tail, in order to keep the slaves indoors at night. A trickle of stories about white manipulation of beliefs in conjuring, witches, and ghosts began to come. It was only the beginning!"[3]

Fieldworkers' reports of their behavior prior to, and at the time of, their initial encounters with those they have tentatively selected for study illustrate the impact of this *rite de passage*. Emotions often surface as the moment approaches and intensify when it occurs, for neither uninitiated nor experienced fieldworkers can ever predict with precise accuracy just what their own and others' impressions and reactions will be. Whether the parties involved are well-known or unknown to each other, and whether they meet and interact in an environment familiar to all

or some or none, they are never fully prepared for the experience of conceiving themselves, and identifying each other, primarily as observer or observed and as questioner or questioned.

First encounters between fieldworkers and prospective informants may be memorable in varying ways and for differing reasons. Fry's experience, as she recollects and recounts it, was
characterized by a fear that she would fail to obtain the kind of
information she desired. So she embarked on the venture reluctantly, anticipating the worst. But her fears proved unfounded,
for what began as a disappointing interview was transformed,
by an unexpected occurrence, into a productive interchange
among the participants.

Napoleon Chagnon, by contrast with Fry, harbored no uncertainty about his ability to obtain information about their
social structure from the Yanomamö Indians of Venezuela.
Hence, he was eager, rather than reluctant, to meet these people, certain that he would find them likable and cooperative and
hopeful that they would like him. Chagnon describes his expectations: "I had visions of entering the village and seeing 125
social facts running about calling each other kinship terms and
sharing food, each waiting and anxious to have me collect his
genealogy."[4]

Chagnon's visions quickly faded, however, as he encountered
his first Yanomamö after duck-waddling through the low brush-
covered hole that served as the entrance to their jungle village.
"I looked up and gasped when I saw a dozen burly, naked,
filthy, hideous men staring at us down the shafts of their drawn
arrows! Immense wads of green tobacco were stuck between
their lower teeth and lips making them look even more hideous,
and strands of dark-green slime dripped or hung from their
noses." Chagnon continues, "My next discovery was that there
were a dozen or so vicious dogs snapping at my legs, circling me
as if I were going to be their next meal. I just stood there holding my notebook, helpless and pathetic. Then the stench of the
decaying vegetation and filth struck me and I almost got sick. I
was horrified."[5]

Once he had regained his composure, Chagnon assessed his
decision to live among the Yanomamö and to study their social
behavior. He reports, "I pondered the wisdom of having
decided to spend a year and a half with this tribe before I had
ever seen what they were like." In continuing, he reveals further

his thoughts and feelings at that moment. "I am not ashamed to admit, either, that had there been a diplomatic way out, I would have ended my fieldwork then and there. I did not look forward to the next day when I would be left alone with the Indians; I did not speak a word of their language, and they were decidedly different from what I had imagined them to be. The whole situation was depressing," states Chagnon summarily, "and I wondered why I ever decided to switch from civil engineering to anthropology in the first place."[6]

Marilyn Fithian was neither afraid of failure nor horrified by those who were to serve as her research subjects. What made the experience of an initial encounter memorable for her was her decision to remove the one perceptible difference between herself and the people she wished to interview. She recounts the event. "There I was standing beside a blue VW thinking, 'What in heavens name am I doing here?' I was there by myself; everyone had taken off," she writes. "Anyway, I was standing there alone with all my clothes on in the middle of a nudist park trying to figure out how I ever became involved in this situation."[7]

Fithian reconstructs the incidents that precipitated her arrival at a ranch for nudists near Palm Springs, California. A sociology student, she had had prior experience as a fieldworker. But she wanted to understand research methods better, and she felt she could do so by learning how to code questionnaires and how to use a computer to process answers. One of her professors had conducted preliminary fieldwork among nudists and had developed a questionnaire he wanted administered. Fithian was familiar with William E. Hartman's research, and she needed a topic for a graduate seminar she was taking from him. He asked her if she would like to participate in the project "since so many nudists had told him that he would be getting a biased view if the research didn't include a female investigator."[8]

At Hartman's suggestion, Fithian visited a nudist camp near San Bernardino to see a play entitled "Barely Proper." After the performance, she disrobed, albeit reluctantly, to join other bathers in a pool. It was a dark night. But being at the ranch near Palm Springs provided Fithian with her first opportunity to encounter nudists in broad daylight and, in the role of fieldworker, to try to get people with no clothes on to answer questions about who they were and why they took their clothes off.

As she stood alone beside her car wondering just why she had come, Fithian surveyed the scene. "From where I was standing," she writes, "I could look down into an area with a cool-looking blue pool with people lazily lying around in the sun. I finally decided I was being ridiculous about the whole thing and I should take my clothes off. To back out was silly," she insists; "it was obvious from my observations of the first few minutes that it was like any other resort with people relaxing around a pool; the only difference was that these people had no clothing on." She describes what she did next and explains how she felt about it. "So I closed my eyes and bravely took off my clothes. I suppose this was somehow symbolic—closing my eyes that is. I felt that if I couldn't see them, no one could see me," she muses.[9]

"As I was standing there thinking, 'Well, now what do I do?'" Fithian continues, "along came a man with a hammer in one hand and a board under the other arm. On seeing me he said, 'Oh, a cottontail.'" Fithian was puzzled and chagrined. "Little did I realize," she notes, "that a 'cottontail' in nudist parlance is synonymous with a white-skinned, non-nudist individual, especially if he or she has some tan which leaves suit marks, or 'stripes.'" But Fithian did not allow the remark to inhibit her. "I decided, 'What the heck, it's too late now,'" she asserts, "so I said, 'Hi,' and picked up my towel."[10]

Fithian walked to the pool area, where she was soon joined by Hartman and others she had accompanied to the ranch. They, too, had disrobed. "Dr. Hartman asked someone where the best place would be to 'set up shop,'" reports Fithian. "He was told wherever he would like would be fine." So they chose the steps leading to and from the pool area, where traffic was heaviest. "We took the material out of our briefcase and started asking people to participate," Fithian writes. "By then I found I wasn't the least embarrassed, and I was kept so busy the entire day that the thought never entered my mind again."[11]

These remarks by Fry, Chagnon, and Fithian illustrate one in a series of confrontations that occur when individuals attempt to implement their fieldwork plans. When the moment arrives, they often discover that they must deal with anticipatory feelings or unfulfilled expectations. Doing so usually brings about a confrontation with self and often results in their questioning or assessing their motives, objectives, and extent of personal commitment. Like Fry, Chagnon, and Fithian, many individuals have second thoughts when the time for implementation arrives, and some even back out at the last minute, abandoning pre-planned projects completely or deferring their research until some later date. If the decision is made to proceed, then one is confronted with the tasks of beginning to function *as* a field-worker and accepting the responsibilities that the role entails.

The nature of these responsibilities is dependent upon the nature and objectives of the project to be implemented. Some-times fieldwork plans call for one to operate as what John Lof-land terms an "unknown observer" and to test implicit or ex-plicit hypotheses by observing others without their having been informed that their behavior is under scrutiny.[12] Frequently this occurs when those who function as fieldworkers select as their research subjects individuals with whom they regularly interact, such as family members, peers, or co-workers. It also often happens when they study people while sharing some identity, as when individuals who fiddle or who practice Catholicism, for example, observe the behavior of other fiddlers or Catholics while interacting with them, or when individuals take jobs as waitresses or arrange with authorities to be temporarily impris-oned so they may observe the behavior of waitresses or prison-ers while relating to them in terms of that shared identity. In the majority of cases, however, the task of beginning to function as a fieldworker involves more than conditioning oneself to observe systematically and to document later from memory what one has perceived. It also entails gaining the understand-ing and cooperation of other people—people who have been chosen, usually without their prior knowledge or consent and often by a complete stranger, to serve as the subjects for a research project.

When gaining the assistance of other people is a prerequisite to implementing research plans, the researcher is obliged to ex-plain o them what she or he wants and, when relevant, the rea-sons for observing or participating in their activities and some-times even living among them. Human beings observe and query each other constantly in the course of their daily inter-actions and regularly generate and test hypotheses about behav-ior on the basis of such observations and queries. But it is neither common nor readily comprehensible to study and be studied by other human beings, knowingly and at first hand, and to interact with them primarily for the purpose of eliciting or providing information. Such experiences can usually evolve and be understood only in conjunction with, or in terms of, familiar social identities and relationships. To gain the cooperation of those they have chosen to study, then, fieldworkers must be able to communicate their purposes and expectations in understandable and acceptable ways.

To facilitate this task, individuals often first present themselves and describe the nature of their projects to persons who can serve as intermediaries between them and those they wish to study. Frequently these persons are relatives, friends, acquaintances, their friends or acquaintances, or professional colleagues; often they are individuals who are known to the selected research subjects through regular or prior contacts or because of the status positions they enjoy. Thus, missionaries, government employees, local religious and political leaders, and community business and professional people are commonly contacted initially; they often agree or volunteer to introduce individuals, either in person, through telephone calls or letters of introduction, or by giving permission to use their names as references.

The use of intermediaries is more widespread among fieldworkers and more crucial for the successful implementation of fieldwork plans than is often supposed or admitted. Margaret Mead reports that she might not have been able to work as she wished in Samoa if she had not had a letter of introduction from the surgeon general of the United States Navy. The man who held the post and who kindly provided Mead with the letter had been a fellow medical student with the father of Mead's first (and then) husband, Luther Cressman.[13] Carla Bianco arrived in Roseto, Pennsylvania, with photographs, tape recordings, and letters from the homeland relatives and friends of Italians who had emigrated to Roseto from a village of the same name in Italy. By acting as an intermediary herself, Bianco was aided, for the senders also served as intermediaries between her and the recipients, whom she wished to study.[14] Napoleon Chagnon was escorted to the Indian village in which he had chosen to work by James P. Barker, "the first non-Yanomamö to make a sustained, permanent contact with the tribe." It was Barker who introduced Chagnon to the Yanomamö, an act that not only provided him with an entrée into the society, but also may have spared his life.[15] R. Lincoln Keiser gained access to a

neighborhood gang he wanted to study through gang members
he met while doing casework for a Chicago municipal court. By
discussing his interests with one of the "Vice Lords" and invit-
ing the man to share his apartment in exchange for his help,
Keiser was able to meet and interview other gang members and
to witness their meetings and encounters, despite the fact that
he was middle-class and white and they were black and poor.[16]
In each of these cases, and in innumerable others that might be
cited, the implementation of fieldwork plans was facilitated,
and perhaps even made possible, by the willingness of individuals to serve as intermediaries and to help others establish social
relationships.

Establishing a social basis for initiating interaction—whether
by oneself or with the help of intermediaries—is essential for
implementing fieldwork plans that depend upon the assistance
of other people. To gain the cooperation of others, however,
fieldworkers must be able to explain their purposes and expectations meaningfully and convincingly. How do they do so, and
what are the responses likely to be?

Consider the following statement John Beattie often made
through the local chief to assembled villagers while conducting
fieldwork among the Bunyoro. "I have come to your country to
learn your language, and about your history, your traditions
and your customs, and the way you live," Beattie announced.
"I have come from a big school in Europe where grown-ups are
taught, including some who will come to Africa. Many Euro-
peans are very ignorant about the customs of Africans," he
continued, adding that "if they are taught before they come
here, perhaps they will be more tolerant and less repressive than
some have been in the past."[17]

Having explained why he was among the Bunyoro, Beattie
next disassociated himself from certain others with whom he
felt he might be identified. "I have nothing to do with the government and I am not a missionary," he declared. "I have not
come here to order you around or to tell you what you should
do." He then went on to describe himself further in terms he
presumably felt would be understandable and acceptable to his
audience. "I have come as a pupil and not as a teacher," he
asserted, "but I can only learn if you will allow me to live with
you and if you will be my teachers."[18]

Beattie's remarks, as he reconstructs them, reveal an underlying strategy that is often employed by fieldworkers and advocated by authors of fieldwork guides. He presented himself not as a fieldworker, researcher, or anthropologist, but instead identified himself in more general terms as one who wished to learn—as a student. Aware that the other whites with whom the Bunyoro had had contact were missionaries and government officials, and cognizant that such individuals had often evoked antagonism or suspicion, Beattie explicitly rejected such identifying labels and the kinds of behavior his listeners might associate with them. By asking the villagers to let him live among them and to be his teachers, he indicated his willingness to accept a subordinate status. Considered collectively, Beattie's statements are innocuous; yet while they are specific enough to be comprehensible and perhaps even reassuring, they are also devoid of particulars.

How did Beattie's listeners react to his remarks? He reports that, for the most part, his statements were "received with amused incredulity. But," he adds, "nowhere was any overt opposition expressed (perhaps because my claims were usually strongly supported by the chief), and in several places people seemed willing, and even pleased, at the idea of having a resident European come to live with them." Yet Beattie also admits that he might have been welcomed partly, if not principally, because as a European and therefore "wealthy," he was regarded as a potential economic asset to the community.[19]

Beattie's assertion that he delivered these remarks more than once—always to groups of villagers and with the aid of their chiefs—suggests that he gave some thought to the matter before he addressed those whose understanding and help were crucial to the successful implementation of his fieldwork plans. Sometimes, however, the need for such a formal presentation is not anticipated, but arises unexpectedly; and a fieldworker must generate a self-introductory speech spontaneously. In his field diary, Franz Boas provides an account of one such situation.

For several days, Boas had been on board the ship *Barbara Boskowitz,* wending his way from Victoria, where he had commenced his fieldwork among the Northwest Pacific Coast Indians, to Alert Bay, where he wanted to record additional information about their language, narratives, and other aspects of their culture. Arriving at an Indian settlement about midday on October 6, 1886, the steamer whistled, and two boats filled with

Indians rowed from shore to meet it. Boas climbed aboard one of the boats.

"On the way to shore I heard them discussing me," notes Boas; "since I looked relatively respectable they took me for a missionary. But I explained to them that I was no priest. I wished to go to an Indian home, and so we were taken to the home of the chief." Men and women began to assemble in front of the chief's house.[20]

"In the afternoon I told the Indians what I wanted," Boas continues, "and it seems they are willing to cooperate. The results of the first day are, of course, not very rewarding, since they must first learn what it is I want. An old man told me some stories and showed me the accompanying masks, which I intend to buy."[21]

The next night, October 7, there was a potlatch festival at a neighboring house, "and of course I went to witness it," writes Boas. "The people were very friendly and invited me to sit down." He then describes the drumming, singing, and speech-making that occurred.

"Finally I noted that I had become the subject of their speeches, but naturally I had no idea what they wanted," Boas reports. "At last they sent a young man who had been in Victoria for some time to interpret for me. I must add that the natives were not too clear about why I was there and what I wanted and they were making all kinds of conjectures." According to Boas, they had at first surmised that he was a priest, but since he had brought nothing, they thought he might instead be a government agent who had come to stop their festival. Both missionaries and government officials had attempted to do this, but the Indians had refused to discontinue their celebration. So one agent had threatened to send a gunboat, Boas informs us, if the Indians did not obey. Aware of his hosts' uneasiness and suspicions, Boas felt the need to clarify his position. "Whether I wanted to or not I had to make a speech," he writes.[22]

"So I arose and said: 'My country is far from yours [Boas was still a German citizen]; much further even than that of the Queen [of England, under whose jurisdiction Canadian Indians lived at that time]. The commands of the Queen do not affect me. I am a chief and no one may command me. I alone determine what I am to do.'" Parenthetically Boas notes that he had been introduced as a chief as soon as he arrived and was so presented wherever he went. "'I am in no way concerned with what Dr. Powell (the Indian agent whom all the natives dislike) says. I do not wish to interfere with your celebration,'" he reports he remarked.[23]

In continuing, Boas attempted to clarify further just who he was and why he had come. "'My people live far away and would like to know what people in distant lands do, and so I set out,'" he explained. "'I was in warm lands and cold lands. I saw many different people and told them at home how they live. And then they said to me, "Go and see what the people in this land do," and so I went and I came here and I saw you eat and drink, sing and dance. And I shall go back and say: "See, that is how the people there live. They were good to me and asked me to live with them."'"[24]

Boas was pleased with himself. "This beautiful speech, which fits in with their style of storytelling, was translated and caused great joy," he remarks. A moment later he was taken aback, however. "A chief answered something or other, but unfortunately they mistook me for a very important personage and demanded a written statement from me that no gunboat would be sent." Boas explained to the Indians that the queen was somewhat more powerful than he, but he agreed to say that he enjoyed their singing and dancing. "They were satisfied with this and promised to make a big celebration for me tomorrow," Boas notes, adding, "I think I managed the affair quite well." He concludes by reporting that the chiefs present told him "that the 'hearts' of all the people were glad" after hearing his speech.[25]

Describing himself and his interests in the way he did was consistent with the nature of the fieldwork project Boas wished to implement. An anthropologist who wanted to learn as much as he could about the culture of his listeners, he had singled out no one phenomenon for investigation. Boas did, indeed, want to "go and see what the people in this land do" and "how the people there live." Furthermore, Boas was truthful with his listeners when he told them that he had not come to interfere in their affairs, but to learn about them so he could tell people elsewhere about their way of life.

Yet Boas's remarks, like those of Beattie, are somewhat vague and evasive. He avoided using such words as *anthropolo-*

gist and *culture,* presenting himself and his purpose instead in terms that were not only general and mildly flattering, but that also suggested humanitarian concerns and selfless motives. Boas did not explain to his listeners why he had chosen to study them (as opposed to some other people), what aspects of their lives he was interested in and what specifically he wanted to know, and how and why he wished to present to others the information he obtained from and about them. Thus, Boas's speech, like Beattie's, conceals as well as reveals; and while both men presumably conceived their remarks to be honest and appropriate, neither apparently felt that he could be, or need be, any more specific for the audience addressed.

Speeches such as those Beattie and Boas made to introduce themselves to their selected research subjects are rarely reported by fieldworkers. How often they are delivered is thus impossible to ascertain. Even those whose reported introductory remarks are brief and direct seem to subscribe to two rules of thumb often suggested in fieldwork guides: (1) avoid identifying yourself with specific labels that may be alien or arouse suspicion (*sociologist, folklorist, psychologist,* for example), and (2) describe yourself indirectly instead by characterizing your interests in a general way, leaving it to the listeners to infer an identity from the characterization.

Frequently, following these rules brings about the anticipated results. Those addressed seem satisfied and gain some sense (vague though it may be) of who fieldworkers are and what they want. Often, however, the nature of the response is unexpected. Boas discovered this, and so have many others, including Robert Lowie.

"A dance had been announced for a certain night, and I made an early appearance on the ground," writes Lowie in his autobiography. He was among the Crow Indians at Lodge Grass, Montana, about 1910. "While I was waiting for the festivities to start, a young man named Wolf-lies-down (as I found out later) accosted me amiably in fair English and was curious about my business. Was I trying to buy horses on the reservation?"

Unprepared for such a question, Lowie did not know how to respond. "I bethought myself of what I had once read in Herbert Spencer's essays on education, to wit, that in teaching a child one should always proceed from the concrete to the abstract; and what held for children would surely be appropriate for aborigines," he writes in *Robert H. Lowie, Ethnologist: A Personal Record* (Berkeley and Los Angeles, 1959).

"So I answered somewhat as follows: 'Well, I am here to talk with your old men to find out how they used to hunt and play and dance. I want to hear them tell the stories of ancient times. . . .' But at this point young Wolf-lies-down, who had never been off the reservation, interrupted me with, 'Oh, I see, you're an ethnologist.' "[26] Unfortunately, Lowie does not reveal his own response to the man's pronouncement.

An experience of Herbert Gans's illustrates that a seemingly innocuous identity suggested by a fieldworker's introductory remarks may subsequently prove to be embarrassing. Gans wished to conduct a sociological study of a suburban development and chose the people of Levittown, Pennsylvania, as his research subjects. "Having learned from previous experience that it is difficult to explain sociology meaningfully to people," writes Gans, "I usually described my research as a historical study." The identity of historian, he felt, was less controversial than that of sociologist, and he anticipated no difficulties.[27]

On one occasion, however, the implications of this label became apparent. Gans was attending a picnic at which a community leader appeared in outlandish shorts. One of the picnickers proposed to a journalist present that she write about the incident in her column. She declined, claiming that she did not work on Sundays. Then she pointed to Gans and said, "You have to be careful of him, he writes everything in the annals of history." Gans reports, "I could only sputter that I was not working on Sundays either."[28]

Like Gans, Richard M. Dorson discovered that being identified as an historian hampered, rather than helped, his field research. Early in March 1952, he arrived in Calvin, Michigan, a rural community populated principally by blacks. "Calvin attracted me as a testing ground in my quest for Negro folktales up North," writes Dorson. "In spite of all the substantial collections from Southern states, no one had ever sought folk tradition from the five million Negroes who now lived in a new black belt from New York to Chicago." By conducting fieldwork in Michigan's upper peninsula, Dorson hoped to obtain answers to three questions: "Had the rich repertory of Southern tales taken root in chilly climes? Did storytelling still flourish as a vital part of Negro culture? How did the folklore of colored families born and bred in the North compare with that of the transplanted Southern migrants?"[29]

Upon arriving in Calvin, Dorson discovered that there was no main street or central business district, but "only a dirt cross-roads where a gloomy store faced a boarded-up town hall." Given this fact, he realized that his opportunities for access to Calvin's inhabitants would obviously be limited. "Two points of contact with the community lay available to me," he writes: "the tavern, a quarter of a mile from the four corners, which I hung around diligently; and the churches, which I attended prayerfully." During a service at the Chain Lake Baptist Church, the minister asked Dorson to speak. In introducing himself, he made no mention of his identity as a folklorist or of his interest in storytelling. Instead, he stated that he wanted to learn about "the local history and background of this unique community," feeling, apparently, that by presenting himself as an historian and querying people about their past, he could get the information necessary to enable him to answer his questions about the tradition of storytelling among blacks living in the North.[30]

In one respect, Dorson's brief remarks proved helpful, for several individuals offered to assist him and introduced him to community officials and descendants of the town's founders. But Dorson notes that several of those he encountered "showed discomfiture at my questions about their past. The township supervisor," he writes, "shifted uneasily during our brief interview" and "dismissed me with 'We're a forward-looking, progressive people here; we don't look back.' " By his fifth night in Calvin, Dorson laments with regard to his attempts to obtain information about storytelling among Northern blacks, "my quest appeared thoroughly futile; the best informed old settler had simply pulled down the county history and begun reading passages about Calvin's beginnings." Once Dorson became more direct and made others aware that it was stories with a past history, and not historical "facts" about the past, in which he was interested, however, he was able to obtain what he wished.[31]

The experiences of Beattie, Boas, Lowie, Gans, and Dorson exemplify several points about the confrontation that occurs when fieldworkers present themselves to those whose understanding and cooperation are essential for the successful implementation of their fieldwork plans. First, they illustrate that fieldworkers are selective when they describe themselves and their interests to those they have chosen to study. This selectivity, moreover, is apparent both in what fieldworkers elect to reveal and in what they choose to conceal. Furthermore, the experiences of these five individuals demonstrate that the identifying labels fieldworkers assign publicly to themselves, or imply through their descriptions of their interests, always evoke reactions and interpretations from those addressed. Frequently, these reactions and interpretations fulfill fieldworkers' expectations, but often they are unpredictable and may result in embarrassment or misunderstanding. Thus, through their self-introductions, fieldworkers influence the ways in which their selected subjects conceive them, but such presentations constitute only one determinant of others' conceptions of fieldworkers' identities and intentions.

That individuals' conceptions of who fieldworkers are and what they want are determined by other factors besides a fieldworker's self-introductory remarks has been repeatedly demonstrated experientially and amply documented in print. As the quotations from Beattie and Boas indicate, anthropologists working in Africa or with American Indians are often identified as missionaries or government officials. Folklorists doing fieldwork in the Southern Appalachians have frequently been suspected of being internal revenue agents sent to the area to locate illegal stills.[32] Sociologists studying the behavior of prostitutes or racketeers are often thought to be police undercover agents or government-paid informers.[33]

Labelings such as these clearly grow out of people's past experiences and are indicative of negative attitudes toward those who function in roles they have learned to fear. When fieldworkers are aware that they are likely to be identified in terms of such unacceptable roles, they often prepare themselves in advance to discount or counteract such identifications, as was obviously the case with Beattie and Boas. But others may ascribe identities to fieldworkers on the basis of their perceptions and assessments of a fieldworker's appearance or behavior as well. Seldom can fieldworkers anticipate what might be singled out and subsequently serve as a basis for inferences about their identities or intentions.

Consider, for example, the experience of Maud Karpeles and Cecil Sharp while they were conducting fieldwork in the Virginia mountains during World War I. Sharp, an Englishman, had long been interested in the folksongs and dances of his countrymen. While lecturing on those subjects in the United States, he learned that singing and dancing traditions which he assumed were no longer extant constituted an integral part of the lifestyle of people in the Southern Mountains. He traveled to the area and uncovered a rich vein of song, music, and dance that he set about documenting. On the occasion under consideration—in the year 1918—he was accompanied by his colleague and friend, Maud Karpeles, herself an Englishwoman. The two had as their objective to record musical tunes.

While working in the Tye River Valley, Sharp and Karpeles were invited to be guests in the home of a local family. The experience was among their most pleasant, Karpeles notes, but it also resulted in an unexpected revelation. "It was here," she writes, "that we first heard the rumour that we were German spies, a suspicion which we afterwards had to contend with in other places." Karpeles elaborates, indicating what else their hosts had reported. "We were told that after an evening prayer meeting the whole congregation stayed and discussed us. It was generally agreed that we were highly suspicious characters and that noting tunes was merely a blind to hide our nefarious actions which included the poisoning of springs among other things." Karpeles states that she and Sharp heard this news not only from their host and hostess, "who enjoyed the joke," but also "from other friends. These included the postmaster, who was convinced that we were not Germans, for he had once seen one, and neither of us bore any resemblance to that specimen of the race. Whether or not they believed us to be spies," Karpeles concludes, "everyone seemed glad to see us."[34]

Such readily perceptible differences as their mode of speech called attention to Karpeles and Sharp and made them seem out of place. Furthermore, an international situation (World War I) had created tensions and aroused suspicions which obviously made these strangers to the Virginia mountains likely candidates for the label "German spies." Karpeles does not consider how their being so conceived might have limited their access to prospective informants, affected their relationships with those they encountered, or influenced the quantity and kind of information they obtained. The fact that they had to contend with the suspicion not only in the Tye River Valley but also in other places suggests that Sharp and Karpeles may not have succeeded, in every instance, in convincing people that it was their love of music, and not their loyalty to the Kaiser, that had brought them to a remote part of an alien land.

While some people felt that Karpeles and Sharp were German spies, the two were apparently never publicly accused by any influential individual. That they might be spies was suggested through rumor. Rumor also had it that John Dollard, a Northern white, had come to the Southern town he decided to study because he wished to organize black laborers. The local people, writes Dollard, "were suspicious of students from the North and tended to think of them as investigators bent upon fomenting trouble and upsetting the situation."[35] Similarly, there were rumors about Richard Dorson when he arrived in Calvin, Michigan. "We didn't know what to make of you when you first came here," the proprietress of the local tavern told Dorson some time after his arrival; "there had been two federal detectives around not long ago, to break up a marijuana ring, and some thought you were from the FBI. But I told them, No, you must be a writer feller like you said," she confided, "because you had those two patches on your sleeves, where you'd worn out the elbows from writing on a desk."[36] For Laura Nader, however, the ascription of a specific identity was not only suggested through rumor but was reinforced through public accusation and denouncement by a respected and powerful individual.

Nader had received a Mexican government grant to support her study of settlement patterns in Oaxaca. An engineer in charge of road building accompanied her to her chosen village, San Miguel Talea de Castro, in the Rincón Zapotec area of Mexico. "The engineer took me to the end of the road and left me," Nader reports. "So began my first field work. As I walked down the path behind two Zapotec-speaking guides," she continues, "I wondered what on earth had brought me to this remote place. Probably as good a reason as any," she remarks, "was that no social scientist had ever before come to this part of Oaxaca to study the Rincón Zapotec."[37]

After arriving in the village, Nader presented herself to a family who were friends of the engineer who had transported her to the area. "After eating," writes Nader, "the head of the household began to interrogate me. Was I a Catholic, he asked. If so, I could remain in their house; if not, I was unwelcome because Protestants were not wanted in town." Nader continues, describing her reaction. "I gasped at the righteousness in his voice and answered that I belonged to the original Catholic Church (Eastern Orthodox). He allowed me to stay."[38]

All went well for Nader during her first two weeks. The people were friendly and the area appealing because of its lush vegetation. But contentment soon gave way to anger. "When two weeks had passed," she writes, "I was summoned to the priest's house, where I was accused of being a Protestant missionary. I felt very angry as the priest examined my letters of recommendation, which included a note from a well-known priest in Oaxaca. His only comment was that the signature looked faked." Nader explains what happened next. "The family I lived with became much colder while the village priest wired the Oaxaca priest, explaining that I had been in danger of being accused. A return wire served to identify me as an anthropologist and a good Christian, and the Papaloapan Commission sent an engineer—as support and as a check on my safety." But that was not the end of the matter. "In spite of these assurances," Nader asserts, "the priest in Talea continued to wage war on me both from the pulpit and in the streets and houses, throughout my stay." She concludes: "There is no doubt that this accusation hindered my work during the first few months and most certainly limited the interaction I might have had with many people."[39]

Frequently, identities are ascribed to fieldworkers initially as a result of single, seemingly insignificant acts. After locating the Songish Indian settlement, for example, Franz Boas attempted to elicit linguistic data from his chosen subjects, a task that was central to the implementation of his fieldwork plans. But he failed at first to enlist their cooperation. "Unfortunately, I had taken a map with me," Boas writes in his diary. "There was great excitement because they believed that the railroad was to be built through their reservation. Because of the map they thought I belonged to the railroad and regarded me with suspicion." The Indians insisted on learning from Boas whether or not the railroad they assumed was to be constructed would pass through their territory. "They did not become any more friendly when I wanted to write down their language," notes Boas. "Not until I became a little rough with them and showed them money did their attitude improve."[40]

Possessing maps, together with other documents, also resulted in the ascription of an undesirable identity for William and Charlotte Wiser. Missionaries wishing to engage in anthropological research in India during the 1920s, the Wisers heard that the villagers thought the male half of the team was a settlement officer intent on checking landholdings and revising rents. "They knew that he was not the district magistrate nor a deputy; neither was he a police official," write the Wisers, who had not concealed the fact that they were missionaries, but who had also not revealed their desire to conduct a social survey of the village. "There had been missionaries here before, and he might be classified as such. But," they write about William, "he had secured land maps of the area and had access to records of landholdings. Who would want these but someone interested in taxes?" Certainly, others calling themselves missionaries had not obtained such documents. It scarcely mattered that the Wisers' assistant tried to reassure the villagers that William was on a helpful mission, for "rumor was against him. They were running no risks with unlabeled strangers," or with strangers professing one identity but behaving in ways conceived to be inconsistent with that label.[41]

Other experiences of the Wisers illustrate that identities erroneously ascribed to fieldworkers can sometimes work to their advantage or even be exploited to enable them to establish an acceptable social base for interacting with those they wish to study. When they arrived in Karimpur, they set up tents for themselves, their helpers, and their two small sons outside the mud walls that enclosed the village. "Now we were ready to study the village," the Wisers write. "But would the village permit itself to be studied? Certainly it gave no sign of welcome." Most villagers remained hidden from view behind the mud walls, and those who did not, the Wisers note, "were terrified lest we approach them or their animals or their children. It was obvious that no one was pining for our acquaintance. And yet our work depended on the cooperation of these, our neighbors. We had to win their confidence and friendship, or roll up our tents and move on."[42]

One morning, however, "a tall figure carrying a closely

wrapped bundle appeared from the corner of the village where the untouchables lived, and ventured across the muddy road," report the Wisers. "He was a Christian. He had heard somewhere that we were missionaries, and he knew from experience that missionary visitors in tents were not to be feared." The Wisers continue, indicating what had prompted the man to approach their living quarters when no one else seemed willing to do so. "He brought his baby, suffering from dysentery, for treatment. We had a medical kit for family emergencies from which we gave him medicine for the baby, along with a bit of homely advice on feeding. As he recrossed the road, neighbors peered from several doorways, waiting to see him or his child collapse, as they have laughingly confessed to us since."[43]

Contrary to the villagers' expectations, the child the Wisers treated did not die but improved instead. "On the following morning we found three daring fathers with ailing children at our tent door. On the following day there were ten, then twenty, then fifty," the Wisers inform their readers. "Half of the office tent was transformed into a dispensary. The previous summer in the hills the Memsahiba [Charlotte Wiser] had heard a lecture on medical helps for those working in villages. The notes from this lecture were brought out and used until the pages were in tatters," write the Wisers. "Our medical supplies were rapidly exhausted and had to be replenished by frequent trips to town. We acquired another tent to be used as a dispensary and established a young villager in it with instructions for simple treatments, while we occasionally withdrew to the office for study."[44]

Their willingness to aid the ill and the success of most of their efforts not only brought more villagers to the Wisers' tents, but also earned them invitations to go within the mud walls to treat the ailing. The success of their planned social survey seemed threatened at times "by prolonged hours of amateur medical service," the Wisers state. "But these hours served our purpose as few activities could have done." The people soon "became communicative, voluble. Opportunities for questioning rapidly increased, although weariness and pity for unnecessary suffering often blotted out our desire to seek information. First aid and home nursing," conclude the Wisers, "had not appeared in our survey schedule or budget. But they proved our greatest asset—and expense."[45]

Experiences such as those of the Wisers and the other researchers described throughout this chapter demonstrate the kinds of confrontations that occur when the time comes for individuals to implement their fieldwork plans. As was true of Fry, they are often reluctant to cut the "academic umbilical cord," fearful that they are unprepared for what they often conceive to be a *rite de passage* crucial to their success or professional acceptance. Like Chagnon and Fithian, they often discover that their expectations are erroneous or that satisfying prerequisites for interacting successfully with selected subjects is difficult, if not impossible. Added to the confrontation with self is that which occurs when fieldworkers attempt to inform those they wish to study just who they are and what they want. As was the case with Beattie, Boas, Gans, and Dorson, they have to decide how they will present themselves and their purposes and what they will and will not reveal, should the necessity or occasion to do so arise. Like Karpeles and Sharp, Dollard, Dorson, Nader, Boas, and the Wisers, fieldworkers are also confronted with the identities others ascribe to them and with the inferences that others make about their intentions. Will they know what these identifications and suspected intentions are, and will they be able to deal with them if they prove to be a hindrance to their work?

The kinds of confrontations considered in this chapter are typical rather than unique. Furthermore, they do not end once fieldworkers have succeeded, in whatever way, in establishing a mutually understandable and acceptable social basis for communicating with those whose cooperation is essential for the successful implementation of their fieldwork projects. Throughout the period of encounter, and even after it has ended, fieldworkers and research subjects constantly confront themselves and each other. Identities and intentions are continuously ascribed, hypothesized, clarified, and assessed. Fieldworkers and subjects are equally curious, suspicious, uncertain, reinforced, and self-satisfied.

Authors of fieldwork guides frequently assert or suggest that there is an act or process that can be termed "developing rapport." Developing rapport, they often insist, is prerequisite for the successful implementation of fieldwork plans. Rapport must be developed, they state, when fieldworkers and subjects first interact with each other. Once rapport has been established they indicate, the fieldwork project can get underway and be completed with dispatch. But the kinds of confrontations that occur at the moment of encounter have no end. Rapport is ever-developing, continuously negotiated, and constantly changing. As is true in every kind of human interaction, as the parties involved learn more about each other, the bases for and the nature of their interrelationships evolve and change. Fieldworkers and research subjects, as human beings, continuously compromise as ongoing experiences provide new data that affect their conceptions and assessments of each others' identities and intentions.

4

Clarification and Compromise

I mplicit throughout the preceding chapter are two facts about the nature of fieldwork that are seldom recognized, acknowledged, or discussed. First, as individuals move from the planning to the implementation stages of their field research, they discover that they must engage continuously in a process of clarifying for others and for themselves just who they are, what it is they want to find out, and why they wish to obtain the information they seek from the individuals they choose as subjects. Second, as fieldworkers interact with their selected subjects, they are confronted with the necessity of being willing and able to compromise. Unlike laboratory scientists, who can control the phenomena that are the focal points of their investigations by controlling the environments and conditions under which these phenomena are examined, individuals whose research plans call for them to study other human beings while interacting with them in nonlaboratory settings must surrender a certain amount of the independence and control they enjoy while they are generating their fieldwork projects. For to gain the cooperation of those from whom they need to learn if they are to succeed in their endeavors, fieldworkers must explain, again and again, their identities and intentions in meaningful and acceptable ways. In seeking assistance, fieldworkers implicitly request permission to assume, and indicate their willingness to accept, a subordinate, dependent status vis-à-vis those they have chosen to study.

That fieldworkers must become largely dependent upon their research subjects is one of the ironies of fieldwork, creating a source of tension as fieldwork projects are implemented. The irony stems from the fact that while it is fieldworkers who elect to study others rather than others who choose to be studied by fieldworkers, it is the subjects who are knowledgeable, and the fieldworkers who are ignorant, about the phenomena or behaviors that fieldworkers decide to study. For their project plans to succeed, therefore, fieldworkers must be willing to learn and subjects to teach; and the pupil is necessarily subordinate to the teacher. Tensions arise because fieldworkers' conceptions of themselves as subordinate to their subjects conflict with their images of themselves as investigators to whom research subjects are subordinate. Dealing with this conflict creates an ambivalence with which both fieldworkers and subjects must cope. This coping requires clarifying identities and intentions for, and compromising with, both others and self.

Feelings of ambivalence that require fieldworkers to clarify identities and intentions and to compromise arise not only from the conflict between images of self as both independent and dependent, or dominant and subordinate, in their relations with their chosen subjects, but also from differences between themselves and their subjects that fieldworkers conceive to be significant. The differentiation may be based on any one of some combination of such factors as sex, age, race, nationality, native language, religious background, occupation, social or economic status, living environment, relative degree of technological know-how, or overall lifestyle. The greater the significance of differences that fieldworkers conceive to exist between themselves and their chosen subjects, the greater the amount of conflict and ambivalence that is apt to arise, and the greater the number of clarifications and compromises that is likely to occur.

The word *conceive,* used twice in the preceding paragraph, is crucial to understanding the points presented. Differences exist among all human beings, of course, but human beings are all also similar. Differences, like similarities, can be perceived or known to exist, but discerned or acknowledged differences become factors in inquiry only when inquirers conceive them to be significant. Thus, there is a subtle, but important, difference in emphasis between the individual who says or thinks, ''They are women and I am a man, but we are all human beings," and one who thinks or says, "We are all human beings, but they are women and I am a man." For the former, a perceived difference is subordinated to an obvious similarity; for the latter, an obvious similarity is subordinated to a perceived difference. Hence, the difference between men and women would obviously become a factor in the inquiry of a fieldworker who adopted the latter point of view because the individual would conceive the difference between men and women to be significant. Such would not be the case with a fieldworker who subscribed to the former viewpoint.

Obvious examples of the two kinds of ambivalence discussed above are easy to adduce. Because they plan fieldwork projects and commit themselves to carrying them out, fieldworkers understandably feel that they have the right to become privy to the kinds of information they set out to obtain; yet they are also aware that their selected subjects are under no obligation to provide that information. Similarly, individuals may determine in advance that the successful implementation of their fieldwork projects is dependent upon their filming, photographing, tape-recording, sketching, or making written records of the phenomena or behaviors they have singled out for study; yet they know that those they have chosen to study are not obliged to permit such activities. Individuals may also decide that to accomplish the objectives set forth in their research plans, they must interact on a day-to-day basis and for an extended period of time with their chosen subjects; yet they are also cognizant of the fact that subjects are not required to welcome, accept, accommodate, or cooperate with them. Fieldworkers tend to assume as well that subjects have a responsibility to keep interview appointments, provide honest and full answers to questions, and submit willingly to any tests or experiments that are part of research designs; yet they also know that their subjects' principal time commitments are not to the fieldworker, but rather to those whose relationships with them are permanent instead of temporary, and that subjects need not tell or do anything unless they choose to tell or do it, regardless of its importance to the fieldworker's aims. In fieldwork involving people studying people at first hand, in sum, rights and responsibilities cannot be legislated by the fieldworker, but must instead be negotiated by fieldworkers and subjects. The negotiating is continuous and requires repeated clarification and compromise.

The nature, extent, and complexity of clarification and compromise necessary in fieldwork can be illustrated best by a consideration of the experiences of selected individuals. Projects carried out by five different researchers will be discussed in some detail. That these projects are in many ways dissimilar demonstrates the fact that the processes of clarifying and compromising are common in fieldwork regardless of the disciplinary background of the fieldworker, the focus of the research, or the environment in which fieldwork is conducted.

The evolution of William Foote Whyte's plans for the study that was the basis for his book *Street Corner Society* was discussed in chapter two of this work. That Whyte's decision to investigate a slum neighborhood in an American city evolved, in large part, from personal motives and experiences has been noted. Having designed his project and selected his research population, Whyte set about implementing his plans. Accomplishing this task, he discovered, was more difficult than he had anticipated. Because he conceived the people of Cornerville to be significantly different from himself, Whyte grappled for an appropriate means of gaining entry into what he regarded as an alien community. He describes and assesses his initial efforts.

"When I began my work," writes Whyte, "I had had no training in sociology or anthropology. I thought of myself as an economist and naturally looked first toward the matters that we had taken up in economics courses, such as economics of slum housing." But Whyte was also auditing a Harvard sociology course on slums and housing at the time, and he decided to do a survey on housing in one block of Cornerville for a term project. "To legitimize this effort," he notes, "I got in touch with a private agency that concerned itself in housing matters and offered to turn over to them the results of my survey. With that backing," Whyte continues, "I began knocking on doors, looking into flats, and talking to the tenants about the living conditions." He assesses the experience. "This brought me into contact with Cornerville people, but it would be hard now to devise a more inappropriate way of beginning a study such as I was eventually to make." Whyte explains why. "I felt ill at ease at this intrusion, and I am sure so did the people." What resulted from this initial effort? "I wound up the block study as rapidly as I could and wrote it off as a total loss as far as gaining a real entry into the district," writes Whyte.[1]

In continuing his narrative, Whyte explains what occurred next. "Shortly thereafter I made another false start—if so tentative an effort may even be called a start." He describes his feelings. "At the time I was completely baffled at the problem of finding my way into the district. Cornerville was right before me and yet so far away," Whyte states. "I could walk freely up and down its streets, and I had even made my way into some of the flats, and yet I was still a stranger in a world completely unknown to me."[2]

The strategy for Whyte's second attempt at entering the community was suggested by "a young economics instructor at Harvard" who "talked glibly about his associations with the tough young men and women of the district." Notes Whyte, "He also described how he would occasionally drop in on some drinking place in the area and strike up an acquaintance with a girl, buy her a drink, and then encourage her to tell him her life-story." The approach seemed plausible to Whyte, so he "resolved to try it out."[3]

Whyte chose a hotel on the edge of the community. "With some trepidation," he notes, "I climbed the stairs to the bar and entertainment area and looked around." There were women in the bar, but none of them was alone. "I pondered this situation briefly," he writes. "I had little confidence in my skill at picking up one female, and it seemed inadvisable to tackle two at the same time. Still," Whyte asserts, "I was determined not to admit defeat without a struggle."[4]

As he continued to survey the scene, Whyte noticed a group consisting of two women and one man. "It occurred to me that here was a maldistribution of females which I might be able to rectify." So he "approached the group and opened with something like this: 'Pardon me. Would you mind if I joined you?'" Whyte describes the response. "There was a moment of silence while the man stared at me. He then offered to throw me downstairs. I assured him that this would not be necessary and demonstrated as much by walking right out of there without any assistance."[5]

Whyte turned next to settlement houses in the area. "They were open to the public," he notes. "You could walk right into them and—though I would not have phrased it this way at the time—they were manned by middle-class people like myself." He talked with the social workers about his "plans and hopes to get acquainted with the people and study the district. They listened with varying degrees of interest," reports Whyte. "If they had suggestions to make, I have forgotten them now except for one." He explains, "Somehow, in spite of the vagueness of my own explanations, the head of girls' work in the Norton Street House understood what I needed. She began describing Doc to me." The woman characterized Doc as "a very intelligent and talented person who had once been fairly active in the house but had dropped out, so that he hardly ever came in any more. Perhaps he could understand what I wanted, and he must have the contacts that I needed." She offered to set up an appointment so Whyte and Doc could meet. "This at last seemed right," writes Whyte. "I jumped at the chance. As I came into the district that evening," he continues, "it was with a feeling that here I had my big chance to get started. Somehow Doc must accept me and be willing to work with me."[6]

The meeting between Whyte and Doc occurred on February 4, 1937. Whyte describes the event. "I began by asking him if the social worker had told him about what I was trying to do." Doc responded negatively, indicating that the woman had only said that the two might like to meet. "Then I went into a long explanation," writes Whyte. "As I remember it, I said that I had been interested in congested city districts in my college study but had felt very remote from them. I hoped to study the problems in such a district. I felt I could do very little as an outsider. Only if I could get to know the people and learn their problems first hand would I be able to gain the understanding I needed."[7]

After listening to the young student from Harvard describe his interests, Doc asked Whyte matter-of-factly, " 'Do you want to see the high life or the low life?' "

" 'I want to see all that I can,' " came the enthusiastic reply. " 'I want to get as complete a picture of the community as possible.' "[8]

While Whyte's answer was not very specific, it probably struck Doc as sincere. " 'Well, any nights you want to see anything, I'll take you around,' " he offered. " 'I can take you to the joints—gambling joints—I can take you around to the street corners. Just remember that you're my friend. That's all they need to know,'" Whyte quotes Doc as saying. "'I know these places, and, if I tell them that you're my friend, nobody will bother you. You just tell me what you want to see, and we'll arrange it.'"[9]

The young man across from Doc seemed overwhelmed with pleasure and gratitude; he was momentarily at a loss for words. Doc continued talking, giving Whyte a few pointers about how to behave on their ventures. If he were arrested in a raid on a gambling joint, for example, Whyte should give a false name. He would be bailed out of jail later by the man who ran the place, paying only a five-dollar fine. Doc warned him that as a greenhorn, Whyte should not gamble.

Whyte took it all in and finally managed to speak. "'You know,'" he said to Doc, "'the first steps getting to know a community are the hardest. I could see things going with you that I wouldn't see for years otherwise.'" Doc agreed, and he reiterated what he had said earlier. "'You tell me what you want to see, and we'll arrange it. When you want some information, I'll ask for it, and you listen. When you want to find out their philosophy of life,'" Doc advised, further defining his role to Whyte and himself, "'I'll start an argument and get it for you. If there's something else you want to get, I'll stage an act for you. Not a scrap, you know,'" he added, setting limits on his role as an intermediary, "'but just tell me what you want, and I'll get it for you.'"[10]

"'That's swell. I couldn't ask for anything better,'" Whyte responded, obviously pleased. "'Now I'm going to try to fit in all right, but, if at any time you see I'm getting off on the wrong foot, I want you to tell me about it.'"[11]

"'Now we're being too dramatic,'" chided Doc. "'You won't have any trouble,'" he repeated. "'You come in as my friend. When you come in like that, at first everybody will treat you with respect. You can take a lot of liberties, and nobody will kick. After a while when they get to know you they will treat you like anybody else—you know, they say familiarity breeds contempt. But you'll never have any trouble.'" Then Doc had a thought. "'There's just one thing to watch out for,'" he warned Whyte.[12]

Perhaps Whyte looked naive or gullible to Doc. Or maybe it was the obeisance that Whyte paid him, suggesting that he saw

Doc in the role of a protector. Or perhaps it was to protect himself from being compromised by Whyte, who, in the role of "friend," might embarrass him. Whatever the reason, Doc warned Whyte: " 'Don't spring people. Don't be too free with your money.' "

" 'You mean they'll think I'm a sucker?' "

" 'Yes, and you don't want to buy your way in.' "[13]

The two men talked a little longer about when and how they might get together. Then Doc asked, " 'You want to write something about this?' "[14]

The question was important, and so was the answer. As Doc would reveal to Whyte later, there were things in Cornerville that disturbed him. At this moment, he knew little about Whyte, but mention of a study suggested a book or a report. A concern with urban problems might mean plans for their solution. Would he write about street corner society? Whyte replied that he would, eventually.

Doc had requested nothing of Whyte in exchange for his sponsorship, except that Whyte not embarrass him as he guided the young researcher through the streets of Cornerville and introduced him to its residents. How Doc personally might benefit from Whyte's presence and investigation he could not know. But perhaps there was a chance for improved conditions and opportunities. Doc asked, " 'Do you want to change things?' "

" 'Well—yes,' " said Whyte. " 'I don't see how anybody could come down here where it is so crowded, people haven't got any money or work to do, and not want to have some things changed. But I think a fellow should do the thing he is best fitted for,' " said Whyte, trying to clarify his own intentions and identity. " 'I don't want to be a reformer, and I'm not cut out to be a politician. I just want to understand these things as best I can and write them up, and if that has any influence....' "

" 'I think you can change things that way. Mostly that is the way things are changed, by writing about them,' " said Doc, who now had a better idea of where he stood.[15]

Whyte's depiction of his early abortive attempts to establish contacts with members of what he conceived to be "a world completely unknown" to him reveals several kinds of conflict that create ambivalence in a fieldworker and that require him or her to clarify and compromise. His initial plan, one can infer, was to gain access to the residents of Cornerville without assistance from others. Yet his attempts to do so through his limited survey work and his brief foray into a local bar made him aware of the difficulties involved in accomplishing this feat, given his reluctance to intrude and his feelings of self-consciousness about being a "stranger" in the community in which he had chosen to work. That his research objectives and plans were also not very clear is suggested by his expression of surprise that one social worker at a local settlement house seemed sympathetic and understanding despite the "vagueness" of his explanations. The woman's mentioning Doc and volunteering to set up a meeting between him and Whyte not only presented a possible alternative means for Whyte to gain initial access to Cornerville residents, but also became for Whyte the way to do so. "Somehow Doc must accept me and be willing to work with me," Whyte writes, indicating his eagerness to compromise and to accept the more promising and comfortable alternative.

Whyte's characterization of his first encounter with Doc and of the exchange between them is a miniature study in the dynamics of negotiating rights and responsibilities. Doc's listening as Whyte described his aims and aspirations in general terms, and his subsequent questioning of the young researcher to determine his specific interests and expectations, served as a stimulus to force Whyte to clarify; the clarification, one can infer, was as important for Whyte as it was for Doc. In soliciting Doc's assistance, Whyte implicitly requested permission to assume, and indicated his willingness to accept, a relatively subordinate, dependent status; in stipulating the terms for establishing a working relationship, Doc outlined the rights and responsibilities of the two men in their relations with each other. Numerous do's and don'ts were specified in the initial meeting between Doc and Whyte. The lists grew continuously as the two worked together, with Doc prescribing the additions until Whyte was well enough established in Cornerville to solicit and heed the advice of others and to determine for himself which behaviors were, and were not, permissible or acceptable.

As Whyte's research in Cornerville commenced and progressed, he repeatedly discovered the need to clarify and compromise. At the outset, he viewed Doc as "simply a key informant—and also my sponsor." But the relationship changed.

"As we spent more time together," writes Whyte of Doc, "I ceased to treat him as a passive informant. I discussed with him quite frankly what I was trying to do, what problems were puzzling me, and so on." Whyte found that Doc was "such a perceptive observer that it only needed a little stimulus to help him to make explicit much of the dynamics of the social organization of Cornerville." Whyte and Doc spent much of their time together "in this discussion of ideas and observations, so that Doc became, in a very real sense, a collaborator in the research." Whyte admits, "Some of the interpretations I have made are his more than mine, although it is now impossible to disentangle them."[16]

Time and experience in Cornerville also made Whyte aware of the need to clarify and compromise with regard to the objectives and overall plan of his research project. "In describing my Cornerville study," he asserts, "I have often said I was eighteen months in the field before I knew where my research was going." He elaborates, "In a sense, this is literally true. I began with the general idea of making a community study." But as he scrutinized his data while preparing to write something in conjunction with his application for an extension of his Harvard fellowship, Whyte discovered that "there were so many gaps that I could not yet put the pieces together." Drawing upon the information he had obtained, he managed to produce two written case studies, one on a gang and the other on an ethnic club. As he did so, notes Whyte, he realized that he "was not writing a community study in the usual sense of the term," but that he was instead "dealing with particular individuals and with particular groups."[17] These experiences caused him to rethink his research plans, to abandon his attempt to produce a comprehensive description and analysis of the entire Cornerville community, and to focus instead upon selected aspects of the social structure. The specifics of the project were continuously clarified and compromises were made, not only throughout the period of Whyte's stay and data-gathering in Cornerville, but even after he left the community.

While Whyte, like many individuals, felt intrusive and self-conscious as he attempted to implement his fieldwork plans, Jean Briggs harbored no such feelings. Studying Eskimos was a childhood dream come true for her, and she purposely chose to live among "the most remote group of Eskimos" that she could "find on the map of the Canadian Arctic." Furthermore, on two prior trips to Alaska, she "had identified strongly with the Eskimo villagers." Writes Briggs, "I had had no problems of rapport, and I expected the same to be true again. Indeed, never having felt very American in my outlook, I rather hoped I might discover myself essentially Eskimo at heart."[18]

Briggs was not entirely without misgivings when the time to implement her fieldwork plans arrived. She was somewhat uncertain how she would fare among a people whose language she did not know and who did not speak *her* native language (English). Like many of her friends and advisers, she was unsure that she would "be able to survive the Arctic winter without benefit of any of the accoutrements of civilization."[19] Of concern as well was her decision to allow herself to be "adopted" into an Eskimo family, a choice that might require compromises which could well outnumber or outweigh the obvious benefits it promised. But as the government plane that transported her to Back River in August of 1963 disappeared into the clouds, leaving her standing on the tundra with the six or seven Eskimos then encamped on the desolate landing site, Briggs had no feelings of intrusion or self-consciousness. She was ill-prepared to deal with them when such feelings did, in time and in fact, arise.

Things went well for Briggs during her initial encounter and early months with the Utkuhikhalingmiut Eskimos. Before the plane that took her to her destination departed, the interpreter on board presented Briggs to her chosen subjects and told them, as she had requested him to do, that she wanted to live with them for a year "to learn their language and ways." She also had letters of introduction, written in the syllabic script commonly employed and read by Canadian Eskimos, from an Anglican missionary and his wife, who were themselves Eskimos and who were well known and highly regarded among the Utkuhikhalingmiut. Reports Briggs, "The letters said that I would like to live with the Utku [short for Utkuhikhalingmiut] for a year or so, learning the Eskimo language and skills: how to scrape skins and sew them, how to fish, and how to make birch mats to keep the caribou mattresses dry on the iglu sleeping platforms." She continues, "They asked the Eskimos to help me with words and with fish and promised that in return I would help them with tea and kerosene." Also included in the letters were comments about Briggs's personal qualities and about the nature of the relationship that should evolve between her and her hosts. "They told the people that I was kind, and that they should not be shy and afraid of me: 'She is a little bit shy, herself'; and assured them that they need not feel, as they often do feel towards kaplunas [white people], that they had to comply with my every wish." Concludes Briggs, "They said, finally, that I wished to be adopted into an Eskimo family and to live with them in their iglus. And in order to forestall any errors, Nakliguhuktuq [the Anglican missionary] specified that I wished to be adopted as a daughter and not as a wife."[20]

The instructions of Briggs's intermediaries were not only heeded, but carried out with dispatch. Before two weeks had passed, she was adopted into a family, and about a month after that, she began to reside in the dwelling of her adopted parents, sharing their single-room living and sleeping quarters and participating in family life. Like the younger of her two adopted ters then living at home (a third was away at boarding school, and a fourth was born after her arrival and adoption), Briggs was given basic language instruction, which included exposure to kinship terms and explanations about the rights and duties of those whose interactions were based upon such linguistic designations. Inuttiaq and Allaq, her adopted father and mother, ministered to Briggs's needs, fulfilling her expectations that as an adopted daughter in an Eskimo family, she would be cared for and protected.

Others in the community were equally gracious and considerate. "When I visited," writes Briggs, "I was given the softest seat, often a seat on the family ikliq [a raised platform on which family members alone sleep and sit], and, like the always privileged children, I was offered milk and sugar in my tea." Similar courtesies were shown Briggs when others came to visit her in the dwelling of her adopted parents. "When I offered food to my visitors, they never took advantage of my ignorance of an owner's prerogatives," she reports. "I was always urged to serve myself first, the largest pieces of the bannock that I hospitably fried were always urged upon me, and if I offered to share a meal with a visitor, the latter never failed to ask whether I had finished eating, before he took the pot I held out to him." Furthermore, Briggs notes, "My fish supply was always replenished before I felt the need, and often even the usual division of labor between men and women stood in abeyance as men offered to fetch me water from the river or to refuel my primus."[21]

With time, however, the situation began to change. The number of special privileges afforded Briggs decreased, and she was not pleased by her own reaction to the altered state of affairs. "I came to expect the courtesies that I received," she asserts, "and even to resent it a bit when they were not forthcoming, though at the same time I told myself that such feelings were shameful." Briggs also "found it impossible to learn to behave in every respect like an Utkuhikhalingmiut daughter." She explains. "Inevitably, conflicts, covert but pervasive, developed both regarding the performance of household chores and regarding the related matter of obedience to Inuttiaq," the male of the family and the undisputed head of the household.[22]

Briggs analyzes the conflicts and enumerates three causes for them. "First was the fact that some feminine skills were hard for me to learn," she notes. Allaq, her adopted mother, tolerated this slowness up to a point, but she also became impatient with Briggs when she did not, or could not, learn, often finding it easier to do for the kapluna than to try repeatedly to teach her. "A second cause of the conflicts," Briggs states, "was that some of Inuttiaq's and Allaq's assumptions about the nature of parental and daughterly virtue were at variance with mine; in consequence not only did I have to learn new patterns, I also had to unlearn old ones." Obeying parental authority unquestioningly created problems in particular for Briggs because, she writes, "subordination threatened my accustomed—and highly valued—independence." The third and final cause of conflict mentioned by Briggs concerns identity. "I found it hard sometimes to be simultaneously a docile and helpful daughter and a conscientious anthropologist," she explains. How much of her time she should spend helping and learning from Allaq and Inuttiaq, on the one hand, and writing and organizing her field notes, on the other, was one manifestation of her ambivalence concerning the identity that should take precedence.[23]

The number and nature of conflicts that caused her to clarify and compromise constitute the focal point of Briggs's book, *Never in Anger: Portrait of an Eskimo Family* (Cambridge, Mass., 1970). Only three of the many she describes in that work will concern us here: (1) those connected with the disposition and utilization of Briggs's possessions; (2) those arising from her antipathy for authority; and (3) those concerning her right to privacy.

As noted above, the letters of introduction from the Anglican missionary and his wife indicated to the Eskimos that there would be reciprocity between Briggs and them: they would help her with words and fish, and she would help them with tea and kerosene. Insofar as these specifics were concerned, the arrangement apparently worked well. But Briggs, like most field-workers who choose to live in remote areas and among peoples whose food supplies and material possessions are minimal, had a quantity of goods more than ample for her needs. Furthermore, the nature of her possessions vis-à-vis her adopted family and the community was an open question. To what extent could Briggs claim her possessions solely as her own, to what extent were they to be regarded as those of her adopted family, and to what extent did they belong to the community at large? The quantitative difference in possessions and the ambivalence about their ownership understandably created conflicts.

Some conflicts arose simply as a result of the number of things that Briggs possessed. The Utkuhikhalingmiut not only live in different types of dwellings at different times of the year, but they also are a nomadic people, moving frequently as sources of food become available in different places. Transporting large quantities of possessions by dogsled is difficult, if not impossible; the Eskimos themselves routinely pile unneeded seasonal items and excess baggage on hillocks or store them in oil drums when the move, leaving them unattended until they return to an area at a later time.

During the early months of her stay with the Eskimos, Briggs refused to leave any of her belongings behind. Her insistence that she needed everything meant that on short moves, Inuttiaq, her adopted father, often had to make two trips to transport goods—one for his family's and one for Briggs's possessions; on longer moves, other community members had to transport some of Briggs's belongings as well as their own household goods. "When I first set out for Utku country," writes Briggs by way of explanation, "I had no means of assessing, rationally, my ability to cope with that unknown and, as I have said, my ignorance of the language prevented me from even questioning the alien judgments of those on whom I had to depend."

So, Briggs admits, "I clung to my belongings with the strength of fear; and, to a degree, I continued to do so until one full cycle of seasons had passed, and I knew, through having lived them, what to expect of the seasons, of myself, and of the Utku." In time, Briggs compromised, agreeing to leave some—but never more than half—of her possessions behind when moves were made. When she was on her way home after seventeen months with the Utkuhikhalingmiut, Briggs reports, her adopted father said to her, " 'If you come back again, bring only a cup, a pan, a teakettle, and food. And if you have lots of money, bring a few ready-made cigarettes.' "[24] In retrospect, the message and its meanings were clear.

The conflicts caused by the necessity to transport and store Briggs's inordinate number of possessions were resolved more easily than were those arising from the rights of ownership and distribution of her goods. From Briggs's point of view, what she possessed was hers, as were the decisions concerning what and how much should be given to whom. But her adopted father held somewhat different views, and the two quickly came into conflict. Briggs's first awareness of this fact came one day when she saw Inuttiaq give a neighbor a can of her tobacco without asking her permission. "I was alarmed," writes Briggs. "If my goods were to be distributed, I wanted the credit for generosity; I did not want Inuttiaq to use my goods to increase his own prestige in the community...." She elaborates, "My alarm was the greater because, ludicrous as it seems to me now, I had the idea then that I ought to do my utmost to avoid disturbing the social balance of the community, the patterns of friendship and of interdependence, so that I could study those patterns in their natural state."[25]

To prevent other such acts, Briggs took it upon herself to offer goods to visitors before Inuttiaq had a chance to do so. She reports that "on occasion, he would instruct me, in the visitor's presence, to give more than I had done: 'If you want to.' " Briggs offers a retrospective interpretation and her immediate reaction to the remark. "In recording this now," she states, "I wonder whether perhaps he was attempting to teach me Utku generosity, but at the time I only imagined that he was trying to accumulate credit for himself, and though I smiled at the visitor, I do not believe I smiled at Inuttiaq."[26]

"Neither Inuttiaq nor I, however, recognized the conflict

overtly," notes Briggs in describing the situation further, "though I am sure he must have been aware of my displeasure, and antagonism generated on this score may well have fed the other conflicts that developed during the winter." She continues, explaining what compromise was made. "In any case, ultimately, without a word being said—really, without my being aware that it was happening at all—we reached a modus vivendi." Briggs explains. "One can of tobacco, one pound of tea, or one bag of sugar was always open and available on Allaq's side of the ikliq, and from that supply my parents offered, or gave on request, small amounts to our visitors; but the storeroom was in my charge." She enumerates other rules that evolved. "When the household supply, the open can or bag, was gone, I was informed, and I brought out a replacement." Furthermore, "When neighbors wished larger amounts of anything than were forthcoming from our household supply, they approached me. During the winter, when Inuttiaq traded foxes," Briggs continues, further describing the arrangement, "he had supplies of his own. These were in Allaq's charge; she dispensed them to me as she did to other members of the family, and while they lasted, neither she nor Inattiaq ever drew on mine."[27]

It was in her relationship with Inuttiaq that Briggs's antipathy for authority manifested itself most obviously. During the early part of her stay, Briggs's adopted father made demands that she regarded as unreasonable. When Inuttiaq asked her to make tea or bannock and she hesitated because she was writing, Briggs reports, he seemed understanding and offered to have his wife do it or to do it himself instead. "Had I been a good daughter," writes Briggs, "I should not have agreed to these suggestions, but I was innocent of that fact at the time. I always did agree, grateful that Inuttiaq was so obliging, and only now do I wonder whether he was trying, by shaming me, to teach me my daughterly duties."[28]

In time, however, requests turned into orders, and Briggs rebelled. Inuttiaq began to address her "in the imperative form of speech sometimes used for women and young people, instead of continuing to use the more permissive forms." When he gave her an order, Inuttiaq felt no obligation to provide a reason for doing so, and he expected Briggs to "obey him unquestioningly."[29] This irritated and sometimes angered Briggs, and she did not conceal her feelings as her hosts were accustomed to do. Instead, she often responded curtly, carried out the command in a way that revealed her displeasure, or simply left the family dwelling and walked alone in the environs of the encampment.

Disapproval of Briggs's behavior was revealed not through comparable acts, but instead through silence or an occasional lecture delivered by Inuttiaq indirectly through the telling and moralizing over a Biblical story or incident. The nature of such responses heightened Briggs's awareness of the contrasts between the way she and her subjects handled emotions. She tried to control and conceal her feelings, but she was not always successful. "No matter how hard I tried to prevent it," she writes, "every now and then, small hostile acts slipped past the barriers I set against them." Briggs reveals her frustration and accounts for the difficulties involved in compromising. "Too late I realized the dignity inherent in the Utku pattern of authority, in which the woman is obedient to the man. I envied Allaq the satisfaction of knowing that she was appreciated because she did well and docilely what Inuttiaq told her to do." She continues, "If I could have gained acceptance then by abandoning my own ways and transforming myself, emotionally, intellectually, and physically into an Utku, I would have done so. But I still had objectivity enough to know," she asserts, "that the idea of 'going native' was ludicrous, that such a metamorphosis was impossible; after all, it was my inability to be Utku in important ways that had created my difficulties in the first place."[30]

Conflict also arose as a result of Briggs's feeling of ambivalence about her dependency status as an adopted daughter in an Eskimo family and the independence she felt she should enjoy as a researcher. As indicated earlier, she often felt torn between her obligation to observe and to document behavior and to help with household and community chores. "After our breakfast tea, when Allaq knelt on her hands and knees to hack away the grimy surface of the iglu floor," Briggs reports, "I lay in bed and wrote, so that I would not forget the events of the early morning. Allaq never commented or criticized, unless the amused remark that she and others sometimes made—'always writing!'—was a criticism. I never knew; the voices were always cheerful."[31] But the ambivalence apparently bothered Briggs, and she sometimes allowed herself to get behind in her note-taking and sorting because she felt obliged to help with household tasks.

When Briggs did attempt to work, there were often additional difficulties or interferences. Because of the comings and goings of Allaq, Inuttiaq, and others during the day, the temperature in the iglu was frequently too low to enable Briggs to type. Her fingers froze, as did the carbon paper. Conversely, when the dwelling was warm, chunks of slush fell from the ceiling, lodging in the typewriter and ruining any work in progress. Briggs's working was also interrupted or halted on occasion because of the frequent flurry of visitors and the family routine. Some compromise was essential if she were to keep up with her work; so she conceived three possible solutions to the problem. She could work for periods of time in an unused nursing station an hour and a half away by dogsled; she could ask Inuttiaq to build her a small iglu to use as an office; or she could set up her winter tent that was stored in the nursing station.

Briggs proposed these solutions to her adopted father on his return from a two-week trip. Inuttiaq agreed with Briggs that staying in the nursing station overnight might not be wise because the kerosene stove there was unreliable. He offered to take her to the station each morning and to retrieve her each evening, but she rejected that possibility because of the amount of time and effort involved. Briggs's asking Inuttiaq if he could build her a small iglu brought a vigorous, and unexpected, negative response. The tent was proposed next, and it seemed to offer a compromise solution. But days passed, and each mention of the tent brought only silence from Inuttiaq. Briggs's initial puzzlement at this reponse turned to anger with the passage of time, and one day she set off walking in the direction of the nursing station, fully aware that she could not transport the tent alone and on foot, but that her action "would be to Inuttiaq a sign, however futile," that she was "in earnest about" the tent.[32]

The sign was heeded. Shortly after Briggs's arrival at the nursing station, Inuttiaq appeared, loaded the tent onto the dogsled, and transported it and Briggs back to the iglu. But he made no gesture to erect the tent in the days that followed. Eventually Briggs worked up the courage to say to him, " 'I would like to put up my tent.' " Inuttiaq replied, without smiling, " 'Put it up.' " Angered by the response, Briggs reports, she asked rudely, " 'By myself?' " Inuttiaq's reply, also uttered rudely, was in the affirmative. " 'Thank you very much,' " Briggs responded, adding, "I heard the coldness in my voice but did not try to soften it." She describes her adopted father's reaction. "Inuttiaq looked at me for a moment, then summoned two young men who were nearby and who came, with a cheer that was in marked contrast to his own manner, to help me set up the tent."[33]

Briggs describes in detail her assessment of Inuttiaq's behavior during the tent incident. Had he thought the idea of setting up a tent in winter a ridiculous one? Had he been insulted that his adopted daughter had made such a bold request? Had he thought that Briggs was dissatisfied living with her adopted family and desired instead to live alone? Was Inuttiaq himself ambivalent, and did he "feel both protective (*naklik*) and hostile toward" Briggs? She concludes that all or some combination of these factors must have been responsible for Inuttiaq's reactions. But the tent, once erected, became a place in which Briggs could work, most of the time in privacy and without interruption, "typing up the notes that had accumulated during the months when conditions in the qaqmaq and in the iglu had prohibited typing."[34]

As these examples indicate, clarification and compromise were common and continuous during Briggs's seventeen-month stay among the Utkuhikhalingmiut. She had no feelings of intrusion and self-consciousness at first, but they had evolved, becoming most intense after she boldly read a letter from a community member to the Anglican missionary stating the wish of the Eskimos that Briggs would leave. The experience had required her to clarify the nature of her relationships with her host-subjects and to compromise with them and with herself.[35] In addition, she had expected to be able to carry out her original research objective—to study the social relationships among shamans—but she had to compromise when she learned that shamanism was not practiced any longer among the Utkuhikhalingmiut, who had been Christianized some thirty years before her arrival, despite her assumptions to the contrary. Choosing another topic for investigation proved somewhat difficult because of her ignorance of the language spoken by her selected subjects and because of the hostility that came to characterize many of her interactions with them. "The upshot of this situation," writes Briggs, "was that the aspect of Utku life most accessible for study, and the one most salient in terms of my personal experience, was the patterning of emotional expression: the ways in which feelings, both affectionate and hostile, are channeled and communicated, and the ways in which people attempt to direct and control the improper expression of such feelings in themselves and in others."[36] Briggs's experiences illustrate some of the effects that the presence of a fieldworker can have upon the people chosen for study, and the clarifications and compromises that those who serve as subjects are forced to make as a consequence of their permitting an individual to assume the dependency status that being a fieldworker entails.

Implementing the fieldwork plans that led to the study described in his book, *Caste and Class in a Southern Town* (New Haven, Conn., 1937), would require John Dollard to talk with blacks. His research objectives were "to study the personality of Negroes in the South, to get a few life histories, and to learn something about the manner in which the Negro person grows up."[37] But would blacks talk to him? And, if so, how freely and how honestly? He was, after all, a white man and a Northerner, and the community he chose to study was Southern and segregated.

Fellow whites were skeptical about the reliability of the data that Dollard could obtain from those blacks who might talk with him. He writes, "They said repeatedly that the Negroes would give me selected information, that, being subtle psychologists, they could read my mind and thus anticipate what I wanted to hear."[38] But Dollard was undaunted. He undertook the task with confidence, viewing himself as a scientist who could work objectively, unencumbered by his identities as a Northerner and a white.

Dollard's initial reception by whites in the community to which he gives the fictitious name *Southerntown* was both cordial and courteous. People were friendly, talked freely about themselves and their activities, and showed "an agreeable interest in the stranger."[39] Dollard responded by being direct and frank. "I put into immediate circulation an exact account of what I wished to do, namely, to get some life-history material from Negroes, explaining that we know very little about how Negro persons mature, in contrast to our knowledge concerning white people," he reports having said. "I added that I was acting in the situation as a scientist and not merely as a member of white society," Dollard continues, "and that my contacts with local Negroes would always be based on my scientific interest." He assured fellow whites that he "would not have come all this distance to fraternize with Negroes" when he could do so in his own hometown. He also "let it be known" that he "was not accustomed to the southern way of treating Negroes," that his "ways were different," and that he "did not expect people to be altogether satisfied" with his actions. But he requested that they afford him "the indulgence usually accorded to the stranger." Concludes Dollard, "This explanation seemed to satisfy people during the initiation of my research, and the plan really worked out quite well."[40]

Early in his five-month stay in Southerntown, however, Dollard discovered that he could not work entirely on his own terms. His identities as a Northerner and as a white were neither completely overlooked nor always subordinated to his identity as a scientist, as he had hoped and requested they would be. Some of the local whites were suspicious of his motives and felt certain that, because he was a Northerner, he had come to Southerntown to foment trouble or to organize Negro labor.[41] Other whites were uncertain about the ultimate utilization of any information Dollard might obtain. Would he write a book? If so, would their views be accurately and fairly represented? Because he was a Northerner, they could not be certain.[42] It was also in his identity as a Northerner, rather than as a scientist, that blacks cooperated with and confided in Dollard. "There is no doubt that they feel emotionally allied with the North and northerners as against the southern white system," he writes, and that blacks "hope for sympathy and support from northerners." Furthermore, notes Dollard, suggesting his subjects' image of him, "Negroes picture the northern man going back and writing a book in defense of their interests; such a book, they vaguely feel, might result in a minimum of force in northern public opinion which might tend to shame or coerce southern white people into making concessions."[43]

That his identity as a white took precedence over that as a scientist was early underscored for Dollard by an unnerving experience. A black man whom he had befriended called on him at his boarding house. Feeling, perhaps, "that the house had become extraterritorial to southern society" because Dollard was staying there, the man went to the *front,* rather than to the back, door to knock. "He was left standing on the porch," Dollard reports, "and the family member who called me seemed unhappy and reproachful. I had unwittingly aided in imposing a humiliation on my hosts." The two men conversed outside, and a second black man was brought up on the porch to meet Dollard. Sensing that they were being watched, Dollard did not offer to shake hands, but kept his hands in his pockets, "a device that was often useful in resolving such a situation." The incident, Dollard notes, created a "strain which informed me that Negroes might not change their behavior toward this house and its occupants because I was a resident there."[44]

Because he was white, and because this identity could not be overlooked or denied in a segregated Southern town, Dollard found that he had to compromise. The boarding house incident made it clear that he could not invite blacks to his place of residence. He also ruled out interviewing them in their homes because, he states, it "would have forced me to run from place to place during most of the day," and because "the poorer informants did not have a room which could be isolated for an hour a day." Meeting at the white school was a possibility, but "the white principal of the city schools was out of town, and his permission had to be secured." Notes Dollard, "Even if it were given, I was not sure that the Negroes would be at ease in the environment of the white school." The blacks' school was also rejected as a possible meeting place because "it was on the outskirts of town and would be a considerable walk; it was isolated; I would be alone there with women informants, which might not look well in the eyes of the community; and, finally, if we had a serious rain, the building might easily be marooned." The town courthouse could serve, but there was too much activity there. The solution to the problem was proposed by one of Dollard's white friends, who suggested that he rent an office "in one of the buildings where professional people were housed. Since it was a business building," Dollard asserts, "Negroes could come and go by the front door like anyone else, and no unusual attention was paid to their movements."[45] So he set up shop there, and the office served his purposes while also enabling him, as a white, to conform to local mores.

Dollard's identities as a Northerner and as a white could

neither be ignored by blacks and whites in Southerntown, nor could they be dismissed by Dollard himself, despite his initial belief that they would become irrelevant once he assumed the scientist's role. He first became aware of this fact through an encounter with "a well-known southern writer" on whom he went to call, carrying with him a letter of introduction. "He met me on his porch," reports Dollard, "and, after an exchange of formalities, inquired what I was doing. I told him briefly." The writer was not optimistic about Dollard's chances "of learning anything about the personality of Negroes; he had lived among them for years and had not learned much; so what hope could there be for me?" Dollard "had heard this before" and "did not take it too seriously." He describes what happened next. "Then he said something, however, which made me angry, but which eventually I took very seriously." He elaborates. "I had the idea in the back of my mind, he told me, that he was prejudiced and untrustworthy, and I came prepared not to believe what he had to say. I assumed unconsciously that he was blinded by race prejudice, as it is called in the North." The writer pursued the point. "I must feel this way, he said, because all northerners come south with this idea, no matter what their formal protestations may be."[46]

Unprepared for such a reception, Dollard quickly ended the conversation and departed. But the writer's directness and frankness had an effect. "Returning to my research," writes Dollard, "I examined the material I had already collected and found abundant evidence of the attitude attributed to me—an attitude which had safely survived my sociological graduate training." He cites from his notes a passage he had written before his encounter with the writer:

> These white people down here are very charming and really exert themselves to do friendly things once you are accepted, but they seem very much like the psychotics one sometimes meets in a mental hospital. They are sane and charming except on one point, and on this point they are quite unreliable. One has exactly the sense of a whole society with a psychotic spot, an irrational, heavily protected sore through which all manner of venomous hatreds and irrational lusts may pour, and—you are eternally striking against this spot.[47]

Dollard describes his analysis and assessment of his own field note. "This excerpt reveals an obvious bias in the form of an invidious comparison of southern white people with psychotics," he states, "and it further indicates disbelief in what they say, exactly as my informant asserted." He also describes the impact of this discovery. "The shock of this experience," he notes, "sufficed to bring about a serious reconsideration of the subject of bias and a conscious awareness of it which persisted during the entire data-gathering period." Dollard explains further, "The example just cited illustrates clearly the sectional bias on the part of northerners of which southern white people are so conscious."[48] The influence of his identity as a Northerner on his investigation thus became clear as a result of the candid comments of a single individual.

After this experience, Dollard discovered that he was biased in other ways as well. He realized "that people were forever asking overtly or by implication: 'What is this particular Yankee sociologist among all possible Yankee sociologists doing down here studying niggers?' " The question seemed pervasive; community whites had repeatedly asked or implied it. "It finally occurred to me," Dollard reports, "to ask myself: What *was* I doing down there?" He answers the question. "Sectional bias supplied part of the answer. I was there on the old northern errand of showing up the evils of the southern system in its treatment of the Negro, and the suspicion could not be avoided that I wanted to make my research come out that way." But there was something more to it, Dollard asserts: "a strong feeling for the underdog, a feeling grounded in my own life history and to some extent previously revealed in self-examination." He describes the consequences. "This resulted recognizably in a tendency to feel with Negroes, to be specially accessible to unusual incidents recording oppressive treatment of them, and to stand with them against the dominance of the white caste."[49] Dollard's identity as *Northerner* was thus modified and complicated by the word *white,* creating the paired identity *white Northerner* and manifesting itself in a form of bias that also had roots in other identitites and experiences.

In the course of his research, Dollard found that other ways in which he identified himself were also sources of bias. "The fact of being a socially mobile person and a member of a middle-class university group," he writes, "inevitably creates a bias tending to make one's research come out in such a way as to be acceptable to members of one's social class; the possible penalty is rejection or isolation by them."[50] His identities as a psychoanalytically-oriented investigator and as a sociologist, he reports, also constituted biases, influencing his perceptions, observations, research procedures, and conclusions. The former led him "to watch for the reservations with which people carry out formally defined social actions, the repression required by social conformity, and, in general, to see, behind the surface of a smooth social facade, the often unknown and usually unacknowledged emotional forces which drive and support social action."[51] The latter bias resulted in his viewing "the community comparatively and historically, and in this perspective it seems historically determined and relative," a "collectivity interacting," with conceptualization taking place "in terms of groups and group relations and not in terms of a specious isolation of individuals."[52] Becoming aware of these biases in the course of his research, Dollard admits, did not mean that he was able to free himself of them completely. "I claim only that some control is possible where insight is present," he states.[53]

These excerpts from *Caste and Class in a Southern Town* illustrate some of the evolving processes of clarification and change as individuals move beyond planning to implementing their fieldwork. Because being white in a segregated Southern town carried behavioral expectations, particularly in relations with blacks, that Dollard recognized as different from his accustomed expectations, he had to decide which set he would satisfy. While his introductory remarks to Southerntown whites indicated that he did not intend to compromise his accustomed manner, he compromised nevertheless by modifying some of his behaviors to conform to local practice. Furthermore, his belief was dispelled that he could transcend his identities as a white, a Northerner, a sociologist, a psychoanalytically-oriented researcher, and a stranger by presenting himself to others and to ego as a scientist. He was forced to clarify his intentions and to consider the manifestations of these various identities in his fieldwork plans and procedures. The introspection provoked by the frank remarks of a stranger sharpened Dollard's awareness of the ways in which personal experiences, assumptions, expectations, motivations, and training coalesce and shape fieldwork projects.

John Dollard's experiences with the citizens of Southerntown
forced him to analyze and clarify the role of bias in his fieldwork, and to compromise with himself by shaping much of his
behavior to accord with the practices of his research community. Obviously, his presence in Southerntown and his
dependence upon many of its residents for the information
needed to implement his fieldwork also required that his selected
subjects clarify and compromise, though Dollard does not
address this issue. But the experiences of John Hostetler and his
associates in one American and three Canadian Hutterite communities illustrate that the compromises a research population
makes to cooperate with a fieldworker, while they may facilitate
the fieldworker's tasks, may also have adverse effects.

An anthropologist of Amish background, Hostetler first
encountered members of Canadian Hutterite communities
shortly after his arrival in Edmonton, Alberta, Canada, in the
1950s. Several Hutterite elders were in the provincial capital to
attend legislative sessions during which land-buying policies
were to be considered that could be detrimental to the Hutterites. Having heard about the newly-arrived professor from
Pennsylvania, the elders contacted Hostetler to enlist his aid in
locating a German language printer. During the period that the
legislature was in session, Hostetler attended many of its meetings, taking with him students enrolled in his course on minority
groups at the University of Alberta. Being present at these legislative proceedings brought Hostetler into further contact with
the Hutterites, who seemed to relate to and to confide in him
because of his Amish background. As a consequence of these
initial interactions, Hostetler not only became acquainted with
Hutterite leaders, but he was also invited to visit their communities. His developing relationships with the elders and with members of the colonies he visited provided an experiential basis for
generating and carrying out a fieldwork project among a people
whom many Canadians conceived to be "a problem" because
of the Hutterites' extensive land holdings, the economic success
of their farming practices, and their self-imposed social
isolation.

Hostetler pondered the research possibilities for a period of
several years, conducting some preliminary surveys on "population change, migration, and mortality patterns."[54] After
examining the existing literature on the Hutterites and consid-

ering possible subjects for investigation, he decided to study the socialization process. Funds were obtained from the United States Office of Education, and three colonies—located in Manitoba, Alberta, and Montana—were chosen as fieldwork sites. Six social scientists, as consultants for the project, participated in generating the research design; selected Hutterites were also involved in the planning and decision making. Hostetler's principal responsibilities were to direct and to coordinate the research efforts of a team of trained fieldworkers, one of whom conducted a census in all three communities while the others lived with their families, each in one of the selected colonies.

Permitting a fieldworker to take a community census and another to take up residence with her or his family was a major concession for members of each of the three colonies studied. A researcher whose three children and mother lived with her in one of the colonies throughout a summer, and whose husband joined them there for part of that time, suggests the extent of the compromise. "There is not room in a Hutterite colony for a long-term visitor," she writes, "and Hutterites dislike prying questions even when asked by fellow members. Their contacts with 'outsiders' are stylized and frequently superficial."[55] Thus, while the fieldworkers and their families lived in conformity with Hutterite expectations, to the extent that they were able and permitted, they were apparently identified as strangers throughout their stay; their presence and participation in colony life were tolerated principally because of the Hutterites' respect for Hostetler, whom they regarded as a friend and as a researcher whose intentions were in their best interests.

That the Hutterites made compromises which had unsettling and adverse effects is best illustrated by an event that was not part of Hostetler's original research design. Early in the period of the fieldwork, Colin Low, the producer of the National Film Board of Canada, asked Hostetler about exploring once more with Hutterite leaders the possibility of making a documentary film about their way of life. For seven years, the Canadian government had tried unsuccessfully to gain permission to make such a film, but Hostetler's receiving the cooperation and support of the Hutterites for his research project motivated Low to try once again, approaching Hostetler directly for advice and assistance.

When Low broached the subject to Hostetler, the latter was

certain that the Hutterite leaders would never approve such a proposal. Photography of any kind was taboo among the Hutterites, and they valued their separateness too much to allow their activities to be filmed and shown to others. Realizing, however, that a film could supplement the description and analysis of Hutterite culture from his own fieldwork project, Hostetler did not refuse Low's request outright. He writes, "I agreed to 'consider the methods of approaching the problem and of bringing gentle and considerate influence to bear on the problem.' "[56] He also agreed to serve as a consultant to the government film board.

"My task as consultant," Hostetler explains, "was to bring the right influence to bear on a colony that would be receptive to the idea of making a film," and, because of the general Hutterite prohibition against photography, "to protect the colony from the censure of other colonies." Furthermore, adds Hostetler, "This I had to do without jeopardizing the rapport I had already established with the Hutterites."[57]

After agreeing to explore the matter and to serve as a consultant to the film board, Hostetler was uneasy, but further discussions with Low and a viewing of some of the government's previous efforts allayed his fears. "After seeing several of the National Film Board films and talking with Colin Low," he reports, "I was convinced that the film board would do their best to make an expert educational film. They were sensitive to the religious convictions of the Hutterites and they would not attempt to film anything on the colony without permission." He continues, indicating specifically what would be involved. "The filming could all be done in one colony but it would be necessary for two or three people to be in residence for a minimum of one month without major shooting restrictions."[58]

Hostetler next had to determine how to proceed. He ruled out approaching the preacher-assembly, made up of the leaders of all the Hutterite colonies, certain that they would not even discuss the project, let alone approve it. He decided to approach the leaders of one colony, realizing that "its members would have to be persuaded to suspend temporarily the taboo against photography." But which community to choose was a bit of a problem. Writes Hostetler, "The colonies I knew that would permit photography under certain circumstances had factional elements within them. To make a film of a colony that had internal problems," he explains, "would be unrepresentative." So he sought the advice of an ex-Parliament member who served as legal counsel to the Hutterites and who was "highly respected" by them because "he had assisted them with their land and tax problems."[59]

The legal adviser favored the project, feeling "that a film would dispel many unfounded fears and prejudices against the Hutterites." He and Hostetler selected a colony whose leader might be approached. This preacher and Hostetler "had become confidants," and the man was highly respected by the Hutterites. Furthermore, "his colony was small, fairly well isolated from others, and he had good rapport with all of his members." Adds Hostetler, "Isolation was desirable to keep visits from other colonies to a minimum."[60]

Hostetler introduced the issue to the chosen colony by sending the membership a letter he had received from the National Film Board describing the proposed project and outlining procedures. He included a letter of his own, suggesting that the subject might be discussed when he visited the colony again. A letter from the legal counsel urging consideration of the project was sent shortly thereafter. On his next visit to the colony, Hostetler found that "reactions were not entirely negative, and the colony agreed to an exploratory meeting" with Hostetler and Colin Low.[61]

Several weeks later, the two men went to the colony for the prearranged meeting, taking with them in the trunk of the car a projector and several films made by the National Film Board, should the Hutterites' interest in the project warrant presenting some examples of the film board's work. After explaining their mission to the colony residents who were gathered in the preacher's apartment, however, Hostetler and Low met strong opposition. " 'We don't want any picture taking,' " Hostetler quotes the preacher as having said. " 'Let me ask you just one question.' " the preacher is reported as having continued. " 'Would Jesus Christ let himself be filmed for a movie? No! We cannot do it either.' "[62]

The prospects did not improve when a large man, who seemed to wield the most power in the colony, entered the room. "After exchanging introductions," remarks Hostetler, "he pointed his finger at Colin: 'Your name sounds Mormon, Mr. Low. Mormons are the enemies of the Hutterites.' "[63]

There appeared to be no hope that the colonists could be persuaded to allow a film to be made in their community.

Aware from past experience that it is customary for Hutterites to begin a discussion by being self-assertive and explicit about their views, Hostetler was uncertain whether the initial responses of their hosts indicated a definitive rejection of the film project. He and Low stood their ground, noting that the government board differed from a Hollywood studio and that the film would neither be sold for profit nor shown commercially for mass audiences. The making of such a film by a government agency, they added, could help to correct misunderstandings about the Hutterites and might even result in improved relationships between them and others. Hostetler and Low also "explained that Colin Low was no longer a Mormon of Alberta, having left his community as a young man," and they "acknowledged the Hutterite contention that the Mormon church owned even larger blocks of land in Alberta than did Hutterites and that Mormon influence in the legislature had helped to form restrictive laws against Hutterites."[64]

The persistence paid off. When Hostetler and Low left that evening, it was with "the tentative promise that the filming could proceed in the spring." Certain rights and responsibilities had been established. "The colony agreed to house the filmers over a period of several weeks while the photographic work was being done. Everything could be filmed except for the religious services." But the projector and sample films that Low had brought to show the Hutterites that night remained in the trunk of his car, for "the colony would not permit the showing of any movies to their members."[65]

The promise tentatively made was subsequently honored. A film crew—consisting of Low as producer, a cameraman, Hostetler as the liaison person for the Hutterites, and, for part of the time, a soundman—worked in the colony for five weeks. Additional ground rules were orally agreed to, and things went smoothly at first. Hostetler reports that the Hutterites "showed great interest in the successful outcome of the film" and that when the processors in Montreal, to whom exposed film was shipped daily, sent favorable reports of the results, these "had a positive effect on the colony members." The film crew and colonists got along well, and the latter were apparently neither reluctant to be filmed nor uneasy when filming was in progress.[66]

Tensions eventually developed. Low became despondent after several weeks, and the Hutterites did not know why. Some thought he missed his family, others thought he might be considering religious conversion and permanent residency in the colony. "The problem for Colin Low," Hostetler notes, "was that there was nothing of tension or excitement in the photography." Low and Hostetler discussed the problem with the preacher. " 'Everything is too peaceful and too wonderful in the colony life,' " Hostetler quotes Low as having told the preacher; " 'if we show this to the outside world they will not believe it.' " But what could be done about the situation? States Hostetler, "We could not introduce any scenes showing dissident elements, colony tensions, family factions, or dissenters. To stage any such situations was impossible." To solve the problem, at least in part, the crew filmed an interview during which the preacher was asked to respond to "a variety of pointed questions about Hutterite beliefs," and they also documented "a conversation between a hitchhiker and the occupants of the egg truck." A cattle branding and a coyote chase scene were also photographed to give "a sense of movement in the film. . . ."[67]

Low's despondency, and the tensions generated in trying to understand and deal with it, constituted one kind of conflict. Another arose because the filming took longer than the Hutterites had been told it would. "After three weeks," Hostetler reports, "colony foremen began to hint strongly that they [the film crew] should leave. This was understandable," he continues, "since the colony was engaging in an activity that if divulged to other colonies could evoke severe censure or possibly excommunication." The longer the film crew stayed, the greater was the colonists' awareness of the possible consequences of the compromise they had made when they agreed "to suspend temporarily the taboo against photography." Eventually the preacher said to Hostetler, " 'Get those people out of here, John; we don't want to get in trouble with our elders.' " And the preacher's son said to his father, " 'Dad, we will have to make a confession after it's all over.' "[68]

The colonists' fear was realized. Members of other Hutterite communities found out about the film, and the word quickly spread. The consequences of the compromise were substantial. "At the next assembly of preachers," acknowledges Hostetler, "the colony was confronted by the presiding elder and was asked to make apologies and not let it happen again."[69]

Other effects of the compromise followed. "After the filming," reveals Hostetler, "I found it necessary to protect the colony from vicious gossip of other Hutterites and from outsiders who wanted to take more photographs." He elaborates, "I counteracted rumors from other colonies that the preacher was offered an exorbitant sum of money for giving permission to film the colony." In addition, he reports, "The traffic of visitors increased as a consequence of the film and newspaper photographers wanted to take additional photographs." But, he notes, "The colony firmly refused permission to let other persons take additional photographs or movies."[70]

Hostetler asserts that his relations with the colony members were "cordial" after the filming was completed and that the colonists "held no one responsible for the suspension of the photographic taboo except themselves." He also insists that following the filming "there was no change in basic attitude or belief" and that the colony "was not disrupted, weakened, or changed in any way." But he also notes that community members "did not allow the film to be shown on the colony"; and, he states, "Even to this day the value of the film is downgraded by the colony."[71]

As the colonists were promised, the film has apparently never been shown in commercial theaters. But it has been aired on Canadian television, and some Hutterites have seen it on neighbors' TV sets. Their reactions, Hostetler reports, have been favorable. Prints of the film have also been made available for purchase, from both the National Film Board of Canada and an educational film distributing corporation in the United States. Whether the Hutterites, whose colony life is the subject of the film, conceived in advance (or are aware today) that the film would have (or has had) such a distribution and viewership is a question Hostetler does not address.

The members of the filmed Hutterite colony were willing to compromise because of personal interrelationships rather than principle. Hostetler assesses the basis for their decision. "I realized afterward," he writes, "that from their point of view the colony permitted the filming not for any of the reasons we [Hostetler and Colin Low] had advocated [at the time permission to film was first solicited and granted] but out of respect for me as a close friend and to their attorney."[72] Furthermore, the consequences of the compromises made by research subjects when they and fieldworkers interact may be greater than the consequences of the compromises made by fieldworkers, as is clearly demonstrated by this filmmaking experience among a people for whom the making of photographic records violates a deeply-rooted religious conviction.

Some might argue that the making of the Hutterite film did not constitute fieldwork. It was not, after all, an integral part of Hostetler's field-based study of socialization in Hutterite society, and the film was not shot in one of the three communities in which the fieldwork for the socialization project was carried out. Moreover, Hostetler himself viewed the film as a possible means of supplementing the fieldwork conducted by the team of trained observers whose efforts he directed and coordinated. The objectives of the filmmaking, however, were the same as those inherent in most fieldwork projects involving people studying people: to learn more about the behavior of selected research subjects; to make records of that behavior; and to present to others what is learned. Furthermore, in an age in which film has become an increasingly popular and common medium for selectively documenting human behavior and communicating its nature to others, differences between the fieldworker and the documentary or ethnographic filmmaker have become more and more arbitrary and blurred. Any conception or definition of fieldwork that attempts such differentiation, either explicitly or implicitly, may be too narrow and difficult to justify.

In addition to illustrating the ways in which research subjects compromise to cooperate with fieldworkers and to facilitate the implementation of their research projects, the Hutterite socialization study and filmmaking venture demonstrate the many ways that fieldwork is a team effort. Fieldwork not only requires mutual cooperation, clarification, and compromise between researcher and subjects, but it also frequently involves the collective energies of individuals to accomplish the tasks of observing and of obtaining, documenting, and analyzing or interpreting information about behavior. Since the three Hutterite communities that served as the field sites for the socialization study were widely separated and not equally accessible to his home base in Edmonton, Hostetler had to depend upon trained observers to gather and record data needed for the project that he knew he could not collect by working alone. Similarly, the filmmaking was a team effort, requiring the services of individuals whose technical skills and know-how differed. Fieldwork is always a team effort in its demands for researcher-subject cooperation, and it may also be a team effort when there are multiple fieldworkers or when the individual who generates the project is dependent upon the assistance of others in implementing the fieldwork plans.

In the case of the Hutterite socialization and filmmaking projects, the research subjects were generally aware of the nature of the fieldwork plans. Moreover, they knew that their behavior was being observed and documented, having given their permission for a fieldworker to take a census of their communities and for other fieldworkers and the film crew to live in their midst to gather and record information about their way of life. This is not always the case. In some fieldwork projects, selected subjects are neither asked nor told that their behavior is under scrutiny, and the identifications and intentions of those who function as fieldworkers to implement research plans requiring firsthand observation and record-making are deliberately concealed. Such was the situation in a study of prophets and prophecies described by Leon Festinger, Henry W. Riecken, and Stanley Schachter in their book, *When Prophecy Fails* (Minneapolis, 1956).

The issue that interested these three researchers was why, when prophesied events do not occur, prophets and their followers frequently retain their faith in the validity of the prophecies or the credibility of the prophesying process, despite the fact that their beliefs are neither confirmed nor reinforced. Published literature on the subject led them to hypothesize that belief may persist even when prophecies fail because the failure is rationalized or denied; the belief is more likely to be maintained, and may even be strengthened, if prophets and their supporters are able to attract other believers to their ranks despite the fact that prophesied events do not occur as predicted.[73]

While such an hypothesis seemed justified, based upon their analysis of documents about messianic movements and prophecies from the past, Festinger, Riecken, and Schachter were anxious to test it in a contemporary context. Such an opportunity would enable them to generate a more comprehensive data base than is usually available in historical documents, they felt, particularly if they could obtain information about the behavior of a prophet and her or his followers both before and after the predicted time of the prophesied event. Any prophesy made, they assumed, would not be fulfilled. Having observers on hand to document the events that transpired prior to, at the time of, and following the disconfirmation would provide the kind of information needed to test their hypothesis directly.

The opportunity arose when the researchers learned, from a newspaper report in late September, that a woman, whom they identify fictitiously as *Mrs. Marian Keech* of a community identified fictitiously as *Lake City,* had prophesied that Lake City, as well as much of the Western Hemisphere, would be destroyed by a flood at dawn on December 21. The newspaper account indicated that Mrs. Keech was not the source of the prophecy, but that it was contained in a number of messages she had "received by automatic writing" from "superior beings from a planet called 'Clarion.'" During their visits to earth in their flying saucers, the story characterized Mrs. Keech as having said, these space people had "observed fault lines in the earth's crust that foretoken the deluge." In their messages to earth, the beings from outer space specified not only the precise date of the deluge, but also the parts of the two western continents that would be destroyed. "The story went on to report briefly the origin of Mrs. Keech's experiences and to quote several messages that seemed to indicate she had been chosen as a person to learn and transmit teachings from the 'superior beings.'"[74]

Convinced that this prophecy of a particular event might serve to test their hypothesis, the three researchers decided to investigate the matter. One telephoned Mrs. Keech from Minneapolis, telling her that he was in Lake City at that moment on a business trip, that he had read the newspaper story, and that he was interested in learning more. The woman was apparently unwilling to answer many questions or to elaborate over the phone, but she agreed to the caller's suggestion that he visit her personally during some future business trip to Lake City.

Two of the researchers went to that community about ten days later, hoping to talk with Mrs. Keech and "to learn whether there were other convinced persons in her orbit of influence, whether they too believed in the specific prediction, and what commitments of time, energy, reputation, or material possessions they might be making in connection with the prediction." During the first of two three-hour meetings held on that day, one of the researchers went to call on Mrs. Keech alone. He "represented himself to be a businessman who had occasion to travel a good deal," and he told the woman "that he and several of his friends had an 'informal group' in Minneapolis that frequently 'got together and discussed saucers and things like that.'"[75]

Mrs. Keech, the researchers note, "was quite receptive, friendly, and talkative," describing her automatic writing experiences and reading some of the messages she had received. But she was "reluctant to say much about the flood prediction and had to be questioned extensively before much information emerged." However, Mrs. Daisy Armstrong, who was visiting Mrs. Keech from out of town and who was present during the meeting, provided additional information, including mention of a group of believers called the Seekers that met regularly in her home community of Collegeville. Her doctor-husband was the leader of the group.[76]

The second researcher joined the first for an evening interview. He was introduced to Mrs. Keech and Mrs. Armstrong "as a business associate from Minneapolis." When the meeting ended, the two men requested and received permission to visit both Mrs. Keech in Lake City and Dr. and Mrs. Armstrong in Collegeville, should they wish more information. Shortly thereafter, one of the researchers made a trip to the Armstrong residence, and he discovered that there were believers in the prophecy in Collegeville as well as in Lake City. On the basis of these exploratory meetings, Festinger, Riecken, and Schachter decided that they could, indeed, test their views by studying the phenomenon evolving as a result of Mrs. Keech's making others aware of a prophecy that she had received from beings in outer space and that she was transmitting to other earthlings as instructed.

"In our very first contact with the central figures of the group," write the three researchers, "their secrecy and general attitude toward nonbelievers made it clear that a study could not be conducted openly." So they decided that their investigation would have to be carried out "without either the knowledge or the consent of the group members." As was noted above, the researchers presented themselves initially as businessmen with an interest in "saucers and things like that." These identities were maintained during subsequent interactions with Mrs. Keech, the Armstrongs, and others whom they met in Lake City and Collegeville. The researchers also hired individuals to serve as day-to-day observers for the project, and these observers were instructed to pose "as ordinary members who believed as the others did" and to try "to be nondirective, sympathetic listeners, passive participants who were inquisitive and eager to learn whatever others might want to tell" them. In describing some of the problems presented by this situation, Festinger, Riecken, and Schachter reveal how actions of the fieldworkers not only reinforced believers' faith in the prophecy, but also contributed to the conviction that those who believed would be contacted by the superior beings from outer space and whisked away from earth in flying saucers in time to be saved from the flood that was prophesied.[77]

One of the hired observers, a male college student majoring in sociology, was instructed by the researchers to attend meetings of the Seekers in Collegeville and "to attempt to get on good terms with Dr. Armstrong, with the aim of being invited to one of the Sunday afternoon meetings of the 'advanced' Seekers." The young man's initial attempts were unsuccessful, and the researchers were concerned. "Time was passing and we were losing opportunities for valuable observation." So they "decided upon a stratagem suggested to us by Dr. Armstrong's inquiry to our observer as to whether he had ever had any 'psychic experiences.' . . . We decided to equip our representative with an 'experience' with the supernatural."[78]

The basis for the created experience was a folktale about a vanishing hitchhiker. Since Dr. Armstrong knew that the student had traveled in Mexico, that country was used as the setting. As instructed, the observer told the doctor that while he and a friend were driving in Mexico, they offered an old woman a ride. She sat in the back seat of the car, and as they drove along she spoke of disastrous events to come. The two ignored the woman, who eventually became silent. When they arrived in the next town and asked her where they should drop her off, the woman was gone. They had heard no sounds of a door opening or closing, and they had never stopped or reduced their speed after they had picked the woman up. She seemed to them to have simply vanished.[79]

"Dr. Armstrong's interest was immediately aroused," report

the researchers, "and he very quickly began to manifest much more friendliness toward our observer, and interest in him." As they had hoped, the student "was invited to attend the next meeting of the Seekers at Dr. Armstrong's home," a feat which made it possible for him to observe and report on the behavior of those personally selected by the doctor because of his conviction that their beliefs in the prophecy and related phenomena were sincere.[80]

The researchers also created a psychic experience for a female observer, whose initial task was also to win acceptance from the Armstrongs so she could be present at meetings in their home to observe and report on the activities of the inner circle of believers. Her experience, she was instructed to say, had occurred as a dream, which was related in the following manner: " 'I was standing on the side of a hill. It wasn't a mountain, yet it wasn't exactly a hill; and I looked up and there was a man standing on top of the hill with a light all around him. There were torrents of water, raging water all around, and the man reached down and lifted me up, up out of the water. I felt safe.' "[81]

The story brought an immediate and positive response from Mrs. Armstrong, who was at home alone when the girl came to call, and from Dr. Armstrong when the observer told it to him upon his return to the house. The dreamer was asked to relate the experience to others in the Collegeville group and to tape record it for believers in Lake City. Not only was the young woman immediately accepted into the group on the basis of her description of the dream, but she was also told about the prophecy and the messages from the beings in outer space. The story had been convincing, and the objectives for reporting the dream had been accomplished.

There were unexpected consequences, however. "Unhappily, it had been too successful," the researchers confess, "for, in our effort to tailor a story to fit the beliefs of the members of the group, and thus gain their approval for our observers, we had done too well." They explain the effects of their strategy. "We had unintentionally reinforced their beliefs that the Guardians [the 'superior beings' from outer space] were watching over humanity and were 'sending' chosen people for special instruction about the cataclysm and the belief system."[82]

The researchers also selected two individuals to become observers in Lake City. Both were to make their initial contacts with Mrs. Keech. Whether because of the experiences of the Collegeville observers or for some other unspecified reason, neither was instructed to tell Mrs. Keech anything that seemed to warrant symbolic interpretation. The woman observer simply told Mrs. Keech that at a recent meeting in her neighborhood "of people interested in ethical and religious problems," the subject of flying saucers had come up. A man sitting next to her had told her that if she wanted to pursue the subject further, she should contact Mrs. Keech, whose address the man had given her. She had come, the woman told Mrs. Keech, "on impulse," feeling self-conscious about doing so because she had no specific reason for visiting except for a curiosity about flying saucers.[83]

The male observer sent to contact Mrs. Keech in Lake City told an equally undramatic tale. He had, he said, seen the September news report on the prophecy and wanted to know more, but he had put off calling on Mrs. Keech because he did not know just what he wanted to learn. He still was not certain, but he had decided to seek her out anyway.[84]

Mrs. Keech reportedly received each of the two observers warmly. She spoke to them freely about her automatic writing and the communications with the outer space beings. She also invited both to return when they wished, an act that fulfilled the principal aim of the observers' initial visits to her home.

Festinger, Riecken, and Schachter expected no consequences of these visits. The observers' explanations for calling on Mrs. Keech, it seemed to the three researchers, would arouse no suspicions or have any effect upon the behavior or activities of group members. Yet as was true in the Collegeville case, the unexpected did occur. "In spite of the relatively ordinary, non-exotic stories that the Lake City observers told Mrs. Keech," the researchers report, "she subsequently made much the same use of their appearance on her doorstep as the Armstrongs had with the Collegeville observers." They continue, noting that "within a week of the first observer's call, Mrs. Keech was explaining to other members of the group that a girl had come to her door, upset, excited, wringing her hands, and so terrified that she could not speak; the girl had not known why she had come, and obviously she had been 'sent' by the Guardians." The male observer's visit also brought an unanticipated reaction, for Mrs. Keech added that "a man had also called, again not knowing why he was there, confused, upset, and unsure of his errand."[85]

The Collegeville believers learned of the two visitors in Lake City, just as Mrs. Keech and her followers had been told about the two who had called on the Armstrongs. "In both cases," remark Festinger, Riecken, and Schachter, "the visits were given as illustrations that 'strange things are happening.'" The unexpected addition of four individuals to their ranks within a period of ten days was a further sign to the believers, not only of the accuracy of the prophecy, but of the fact that the superior beings from outer space had selected them for salvation from the cataclysm and for important responsibilities following the predicted event.[86]

Having won acceptance into the Lake City and Collegeville groups, the four observers became active participants in the believers' activities, making notes on their observations whenever they could do so unnoticed, and tape recording their experiences in a hotel room rented for that purpose after the two groups of believers joined in Lake City shortly before the prophesied flood. Because the number, length, and intensity of meetings rapidly increased as the fated day approached, the observers were almost constantly in the homes of the Armstrongs or Mrs. Keech, interacting closely and continuously with those who had banded together for the common cause.

Because of the demands made on their time and the participation required to maintain their credibility as sincere believers, the observers were not always able to maintain complete neutrality, report Festinger, Riecken, and Schachter. The four sometimes had to compromise. When differences of opinion arose among group members, for example, the observers were sometimes forced to take a stand, and they occasionally had to share the responsibilities of responding to queries from "outsiders" who telephoned the Keech residence. Some were also prepared to quit their jobs in preparation for the deluge, as other group members had done, and while none of the observers actually did so, one stretched the truth and indicated on December 17 "that her job had been terminated." A Collegeville observer found it impossible to refuse a request from the Armstrongs to remain in their home and help care for their children while the couple went off to Lake City to visit Mrs. Keech and to participate in group meetings at her house.[87]

The observation for the project lasted from November 19 to January 7, report the researchers. The outer space visitors who, according to messages Mrs. Keech received through automatic writing, were to pick up the believers in flying saucers failed on three specific occasions to do so. December 21 came and went, and the predicted flood did not occur. But the believers were undaunted, convinced from yet other messages that space beings had been among them and that their faith had been responsible for the cancellation of the cataclysm. The appearance of yet another hired observer on Christmas Day further bolstered belief, "for he was the only new recruit the group attracted" after the prophecy had been disconfirmed. "Our data, in places, are less complete than we would like," conclude Festinger, Riecken, and Schachter, and "our influence on the group somewhat greater than we would like. We were able, however," they remark, "to collect enough information to tell a coherent story and, fortunately, the effects of the disconfirmation were striking enough to provide for firm conclusions."[88]

Some of the compromises required of the hired observers were noted above. Festinger, Riecken, and Schachter also had to compromise. Given the short amount of time available for a fieldwork project after they learned of the prophecy and determined it could serve as a basis for testing their views, they had to generate strategies which they might not have utilized had time and circumstances permitted alternative research procedures. The experiences of those involved in the prophecy project best illustrate the fact that research subjects are often compromised, even when preventive efforts are made. The behavior of the fieldworkers in their relations with the subjects inadvertently provided reinforcement, and perhaps even the principal impetus, for a movement that raised human hopes to a feverish pitch and that had unanticipated, and perhaps unpredictable, consequences for the individuals who became caught up in it.

In some respects the five fieldwork projects described above seem incompatible. Those who generated and carried out the projects are professionally diverse; the objectives of their studies, their selected research subjects, the settings in which they worked, and the foci of their investigations differ considerably. Yet taken collectively, the five projects illustrate the processes of clarification and compromise that evolve when fieldwork plans are implemented, and they reveal how and why all the individuals involved in any given fieldwork project affect, and are affected by, the behavior of one another. The five projects also exemplify the variety and complexity of clarification and compromise, and they suggest the kinds of consequences that follow from the decisions made.

Despite their usefulness, when considered collectively, to suggest a broad spectrum of clarifications and compromises, the experiences of the five researchers do not exhaust the range of possibilities. None illustrates the fact that while individuals are implementing their fieldwork plans, they often find it necessary to clarify for family, friends, and acquaintances who are not directly involved in the research just what they are doing with their time, energies, and resources, and why they have chosen to study certain phenomena or individuals. Moreover, none of the projects discussed demonstrates the frequent need for compromise by those who regularly interact with fieldworkers as the research evolves and the fieldworkers have less time to devote to them and to matters of mutual interest. Finally, none of the five fieldwork projects described above considers in any detail the clarifying and compromising, with others and self, that occur after the firsthand interaction between fieldworker and research subject ends.

5

Reflection
and Introspection

Robert read the book slowly and with feeling, pausing only occasionally to take a swig of gin and chase it quickly with some beer," writes Elliot Liebow. "Lonny listened quietly and watched with blinking eyes as Robert changed his voice for each of the characters, assuming a falsetto for Snow White. But my own interest started to wander, probably because I had already read the book and seen the movie," notes Liebow, describing a memorable moment during his fieldwork among blacks in a poor neighborhood of Washington, D.C., early in the 1960s.[1]

"Suddenly Robert raised his voice and startled me back into attention," continues Liebow, revealing what happened next. "I looked at Lonny—placid, eye-blinking Lonny—and at Ronald—a handkerchief around his head and a gold earring stuck in his left ear making him look like a storybook pirate— and wondered what the hell I was doing there with these two guys, drinking gin and beer and listening to *Snow White and the Seven Dwarfs.*"[2]

The questions pondered by Liebow (Why am I where I am? Why am I doing what I am doing? Why am I with the people I am with?) are common and recurrent among individuals who assume the fieldworker's role. Of those whose fieldwork experiences have been mentioned or described thus far, those who report having asked such questions of themselves include Peggy Golde, Marilyn Fithian, Napoleon Chagnon, and Laura Nader.

Such questions come to mind when fieldworkers realize that the environments in which they find themselves, the behaviors they observe and often attempt to imitate, or the individuals with whom they are interacting seem to differ in striking ways from familiar places, activities, or people. These "why" questions arose for Golde as she was riding up a narrow mountain path on the back of a mule toward an isolated Mexican Indian village, for Fithian as she stood fully clothed beside her Volkswagen in the parking lot of a nudist camp near Palm Springs, for Chagnon as he came face to face for the first time with the unsightly Yanomamö Indians in a Venezuelan jungle, for Nader as she walked along behind two Zapotec-speaking guides on a deserted path leading to a remote town in Oaxaca, and for Liebow as he sat with a small group of adult men in the midst of an urban ghetto drinking a combination of alcholic beverages and listening to a reading of a well-known fairy tale. For each of these individuals, and for fieldworkers in general, posing "why" questions to self is one manifestation of the recurring reflection and introspection common during fieldwork experiences.

Reflection and introspection are integral to human existence, occurring continuously throughout the lifetime of every human being. We not only act, but we also reflect upon our actions as well as those of other people, and reflection often leads to introspection. Reflection and introspection tend to be more frequent and intense when we are exposed to unfamiliar or unexpected stimuli, and when our responses to those stimuli make us aware of contrasts between past and present experiences or between expectations and actualities. Fieldworkers channel their efforts to achieve goals that demand the amassing of information about the behavior of other human beings. Therefore, the frequency and intensity of reflection and introspection tend to be greater during periods of fieldwork than is the case at other times.

Frequently, awareness of contrasts between fieldwork and habitual experience causes individuals to reflect upon and to long for customary modes they have taken for granted. This is most common, perhaps, when circumstances make it impossible for fieldworkers to satisfy basic needs in accustomed ways or to enjoy personal privacies to which they feel they are entitled. "We found it inhibiting," writes Robert K. Dentan about his and his wife's fieldwork among the Semai of Malaysia, for example, "when trying to indulge in a little connubial bliss in our creaky house, when Uproar, our next door neighbor, would shout jokingly, 'Hey, what are you two doing in there?' " Dentan provides a second example. "Similarly, I found it hard to adapt to the fact that going to the river to defecate meant answering cries of 'Where are you going?' The evasive answer, 'To the river,' merely led people to ask, 'Why are you going to the river?' A mumbled, 'To defecate' brought a reply of either, 'Have a good defecation' or, sometimes, if the speaker was a man, 'Hang on, I'll come with you.' To reject this proffered companionship," notes Dentan, "would have risked ruining our relationship." Dentan's wife, Ruth, found the women equally gregarious when it came to the act of elimination. "We squat there in a row in the water, with our sarongs up, like a bunch of ducks." The Dentans' partial solution to the problem of how to maintain some degree of accustomed privacy was to establish a "taboo day" each week on which they were "ritually unable" to do much socializing. It was then that they found it possible to read, sleep, and write letters with fewer interruptions.[3]

While conducting fieldwork in Japan, Edward Norbeck and his wife similarly failed repeatedly in their attempts to be alone. "A long trip by rowboat to a barren rocky islet brought us face to face with a large troupe of Japanese picnickers," writes Norbeck, and even when the couple sought isolation on what seemed to be deserted beaches or remote mountain-tops, "people always appeared soon after our arrival." Only once did the Norbecks succeed when, on a frosty morning that kept most sightseers indoors, they chartered a bus for themselves, traveled to a volcanic mountain, and walked together through snow from the end of the road to the volcano's edge. "We were alone at last," Norbeck states.[4]

Many fieldworkers have had to reconcile themselves to the unaccustomed sight of seething waves of maggots in the waste facilities or to the existence of makeshift sanitation and limited opportunities for bathing.[5] Nearly as disconcerting, and often mentioned in the same breath, is the matter of diet. While doing fieldwork in Nepal, writes John T. Hitchcock, he and his family had such a range of foodstuffs as "parched soybeans, boiled potatoes, two varieties of popped maize, including ordinary field maize," on which, he reports, he "broke two teeth."[6]

Norma Diamond also found contrasts in food a subject for reflection and "the chief source of culture shock" for her. "I was grateful," Diamond asserts, "that villagers concerned about my well-being would ask 'Can you eat Taiwanese food?' rather than 'Do you like Taiwanese food?' Except for the dishes served at festivals, weddings, and funerals," she confesses, "I would have been hard put to give a convincing 'yes' to the second question."[7]

Differences in diet also constituted problems for Jean Briggs while she lived among the Eskimos. "It was hard to accustom myself to a diet of raw fish, eaten skin, scales, and all," Briggs reports. "I never did succeed in mastering the skin, but at first I tried, valiantly, though the scales stuck in my throat and the slime made me retch." Fish was usually plentiful, so she was rarely hungry. But Briggs craved foods such as oatmeal, dates, and boiled rice; "much of the time my secret thoughts crept guiltily around one problem," she reveals, namely, "how best to create opportunities for gorging myself on these familiar foods without having to share them with the visitors who were so generous with their own food." Concerned that she might not be able to remain healthy, or perhaps even survive, solely on an Eskimo diet, Briggs eventually rationed out her limited quantities of familiar foods over a period of time to ensure continuous supplementation of the native fare. The absurdity of such an act became apparent to Briggs only after her Arctic adventure had ended. "Unpacking on my return," she notes, "I was amazed to find eight sesame seeds that I had hoarded, carefully wrapped in tinfoil, for an emergency; whenever I failed to make myself understood; when Saarak [one of the children of the family into which Briggs was adopted] wailed at the sight of me; or when the cries of the seagulls reminded me of home, my solace was food."[8]

In addition to, and sometimes because of, their reflections on contrasts between their fieldwork and other experiences, fieldworkers often suffer spiritual discomfiture and feelings of intellectual deprivation. While studying the Trobriand Islanders, Bronislaw Malinowski worked desultorily on a tortoise shell belt, read "trashy" magazines, took frequent naps, and attempted (apparently without much success) to repress "lustful thoughts" of his fiancée, who was not with him, and of the native women who surrounded him.[9] Franz Boas not only cherished the letters he received from his wife and parents while he was conducting fieldwork among the Northwest Pacific Coast Indians during the closing decades of the nineteenth century, but he also wrote to them frequently, revealing his loneliness and reiterating his desire to finish his work quickly so he could be reunited with his family and return to familiar surroundings.[10] A major source of frustration for Margaret Mead during her initial fieldwork venture was the inaccessibility of professional colleagues with whom she could discuss theoretical and procedural problems raised by her fieldwork, on the one hand, and explore the significance and implications of the data she gathered from day to day, on the other.[11] That innumerable fieldworkers report seeking solace or escape when in the field by reading novels and magazines, keeping diaries, and corresponding regularly with family, friends, and peers indicates that despite the demands and satisfactions of doing fieldwork, reflection and introspection are not evoked only by, or confined solely to, the scholarly tasks at hand.[12]

The difficulty or impossibility of meeting fundamental needs in familiar ways and of enjoying accustomed privacy is but one spur to reflection and introspection during fieldwork. Another is the inability of fieldworkers to be totally impersonal and objective while observing and interacting with those they have chosen to study. Despite their desire to view their subjects solely as sources of information and their attempts to avoid personal involvement in their subjects' affairs, they discover that they cannot remain completely detached. Thus, when their personal and professional relationships conflict, fieldworkers often become contemplative, pondering means of mediating the apparent oppositions between these ways of relating to and interacting with their research subjects.

Sometimes such dilemmas result from trivial events that are regarded as significant only within the broader context of the overall fieldwork experience. This was the case, for instance, with an incident that occurred while Ernestine Friedl was conducting fieldwork in a rural Greek village in 1955-1956.

Friedl reports several reasons for her choice of a village in Greece as a fieldwork site. She was interested in peasants and in the process of social change as it occurred "in underdeveloped countries." In addition, she wished to supplement her previous fieldwork experiences among American Indians "by doing field work in a setting where it was essential to learn the local language and where the culture and social structure of the society were not dominated by problems of acculturation in an American setting." Greece was chosen both because little field research had been done there and because Friedl and her husband, a classicist, "wanted a year together...." Working in Greece would enable Friedl's husband to assist in her fieldwork and to acquire "a living supplement to his knowledge and understanding of ancient literature and society." Having settled on Greece for these reasons, Friedl obtained a Fulbright research grant and, after consulting with Greek officials and considering the possibilities, she chose to work in a village that she identified with the fictitious name *Vasilika*.[13]

The incident that served as the stimulus for reflection and introspection occurred shortly after Friedl and her husband arrived in their chosen community. One reason for their selecting Vasilika over other villages was the offer of the entire second floor of a private house as a place of residence during the planned period of their fieldwork. At the time they inspected and decided to lease them, the quarters were sparsely, though adequately, furnished, but when they arrived to begin their occupancy, Friedl and her husband discovered that all the furnishings had been moved downstairs because, they were told, the family needed them. Rather than protest, the couple acquired some furniture during a two-day trip. Writes Friedl, "The furniture we couldn't fit into our car was loaded onto a 1932 Chevrolet sedan—the elderly driver being the only man we could find who would take the stuff—and we entered the village in caravan on October 26, St. Demetrius Day." The sight, understandably, attracted the villagers' attention.[14]

"Two days later," Friedl continues, "the twenty pieces of assorted luggage and boxes we had stored in Piraeus arrived." At the advice of individuals associated with the Fulbright program, Friedl and her husband had purchased "enough of essential toilet articles, nylon hose, and clothes of all sorts to last the entire year because such items were either not available or very expensive in Greece." As they began unpacking in their chambers, members of the family in whose house they were settling took turns watching. "We became progressively more embarrassed," writes Friedl, "not only because strangers were watching us unpack all our belongings, intimate and personal ones as well as books and papers, but also because the place began to look like a general store." She explains what happened next. "Then the daughter of the house asked me if she could have a pair of nylon hose, since I had so many. I was startled by the direct request and uncertain as to what to do."[15]

Friedl reflected briefly on what she had read about Greeks. She recalled that "there were many references to the Greek contempt for people who are easily duped." Had she and her husband already been duped once, she wondered, when all the furnishings were removed from their rooms without prior warning? If so, had the couple's failure to protest perhaps already generated contempt from the family? "Now they were asking us to give away some of our belongings," notes Friedl. "Would they lose all respect for us if I said 'Yes,' or would they be pleased? Would a single pair be enough, or would the girl want more?"[16]

There was little time. "The decision had to be made immediately," writes Friedl. She describes the action she decided upon. "I did what was most comfortable by my own standards; I gave her a pair, since I would have felt like a fool not to when I had two dozen pairs at hand." But the gift was accompanied by a verbalized qualification. "I hedged against what I thought were the hazards of Greek culture by saying that I needed to keep the rest because they had to last through the entire year." It was in this way that Friedl resolved a dilemma caused by the conflicting identities of empathic human being and objective fieldworker.[17]

As was true for Friedl, fieldworkers can sometimes generate and evaluate alternative modes of action quickly and make judgments that lead to sensible compromises. Frequently, however, the nature of specific experiences makes it difficult or impossible for fieldworkers to consider subordinating human concerns to professional objectives. When a human life is threatened, for example, and fieldworkers are in a position to protect or save an endangered fellow human being, they usually act spontaneously and humanely without first contemplating the appropriateness of their behavior to the fieldworker's role. The distinctions between objectivity and subjectivity and between the impartial observer and the biased participant have little relevance in such instances. Reflection and introspection may follow, and when they do, the appropriateness of the action already taken may be assessed in retrospect. But it is hindsight rather than forethought that brings the alternatives and their implications into focus. Such was the case for Colin Turnbull while he was studying the Ik of East Africa in the mid-1960s.

As his fieldwork among the Ik evolved, Turnbull learned early that the attitudes and values of these people differ radically from those that are common in other societies. Forced out of their native environment because of the establishment of a game reserve, the Ik wander somewhat aimlessly in a desolate mountainous region bordering Kenya, the Sudan, and Uganda. There they exist as best they can on whatever they can find in a drought-ridden and barren land. The scarcity of food and water gives the drive for self-preservation priority over concern with the welfare of fellow human beings, and it fosters a general indifference toward human suffering and death. In a place of too little, it is the fittest who survive and the old and very young who suffer most.

These attitudes and values conflicted with Turnbull's own, and while he could understand the reasons for them, he could neither condone nor adopt them. Instead, he usually operated according to his own standards, particularly in his relationships with the elderly. He frequently shared his food and administered medical aid to the older Ik, whose own children ignored them and often left them to starve or die unattended. The humane assistance and care he provided seemed natural to Turnbull, though he was reproved by the younger adults for wasting his provisions and time on those they regarded as unworthy of such attention. On one occasion, however, Turnbull wondered, in retrospect, whether or not his actions during that crisis situation were really in the best interests of the individual he helped, and whether the attitudes of the Ik were perhaps more defensible than his own.

The incident occurred when the Ik abandoned their established village and hurriedly moved their transportable belongings to a new site. While the Ik were not involved, their village was located in the area in which two other tribal peoples fought over a theft of cattle. To avoid becoming victims of a struggle in which they played no part, the Ik quickly pulled up stakes, relocating just downhill from their besieged location and closer to the local police post, where some amount of protection seemed assured.

Loading his own possessions onto his Land Rover, Turnbull observed the migration and witnessed the speedy emergence of a new compound as dwellings were reconstructed from poles, skins, and roofs moved from the old to the new living site. As he watched, Turnbull spotted an old man, too frail to walk, dragging himself down the hill on his side. One of the man's sons helped him part of the way, but abandoned him before reaching the new camp when his younger brother derided him for not transporting more useful things. Turnbull intervened, carrying the bony body into the compound, where he obtained crude quarters for his charge Loiangorok by bribing one of the Ik with promises of food and money.

"It was there, while I was nursing Loiangorok, that there was a sudden exodus from the village, distant shouts of laughter, and then someone running back to tell me to come quickly," writes Turnbull. "At first I thought it was a trick to get me away from the old man while in the middle of feeding him," he continues, "so I finished that first and then went to see what the excitement was about." He describes the scene. "It was someone else whom I had never seen before, dead Lolim's widow, Lo'ono. She too had been abandoned, and had tried to make her way down the mountainside." The attempt, reports Turnbull, had not succeeded. "But she was totally blind and had tripped and rolled to the bottom of the *oror a pirre'i*, and there she lay on her back, her legs and arms thrashing feebly, while a little crowd standing on the edge above looked down at her and laughed at the spectacle."[18]

Turnbull describes his response. "At this time Joseph Towles was with me and had brought fresh medical supplies. He stayed with her and kept others away, while I ran back to get medicine and food and water, for Lo'ono was obviously nearly dead from hunger and thirst as well as from the fall. Then a really terrible thing happened," notes Turnbull. "We treated her and fed her, and asked her to come back with us, thinking we might as well start a whole village for the old and abandoned. But she refused, and said she wanted to go on, if we would just point her in the direction of her son's new village."[19]

Turnbull had misgivings about the woman's wishes. "Her

son was the same one who had driven old Lolim [his father] out so that Lolim died outside, not more than a few yards away," he recalled. "I said I did not think she would get much of a welcome there, and she replied that she knew it but at least she wanted to be near him when she died; perhaps when Longoli [the son] saw the food we had given her," Turnbull thought, "he might let her into the compound. So we gave her more food and made her eat and drink all she could, put her stick in her hand and pointed her the way she wanted to be pointed, and she suddenly cried." Turnbull describes his reaction. "Thinking she was afraid or wanted us to go with her, I asked, and she said no; she was crying, she said, because all of a sudden we reminded her that there had been a time when people had helped each other, when people had been kind and good. Still crying, she set off."[20]

The incident had its repercussions. "The Ik up to this point had been tolerant of my activities," Turnbull asserts, "but all this was too much, combined with the fact that my colleague established a dispensary where he treated old people as well as young, but gave food only to the old." He describes the Ik reaction to this. "Openly critical of this waste of effort and food and medicine, the Ik said that what we were doing was wrong. Food and medicine were for the living, not the dead. But the old continued to come, the few who were left, not in the hopes of being kept alive, but so that they could go off quietly and die a little more comfortably."[21]

The experience and reactions to it made Turnbull reflective and introspective. "Then I thought of Lo'ono—that incredibly wrinkled old face, the sightless eyes peering as though they could still, with a struggle, see, and then those sudden, frightening tears of anguish at a memory that had been better forgotten," he reports. "And I thought of other old people who had joined in the merriment when they had been teased, knocked over or had a precious morsel of food taken from their mouths," Turnbull continues. "They knew that it was silly of them to expect to go on living, and, having watched others, they knew that the spectacle really was quite funny. So they joined in the laughter."[22]

Turnbull's thoughts turned once again to the blind old Lo'ono. "Perhaps if we had left Lo'ono, she would have died laughing, happy that she was at least providing her children with amusement. But what did we do?'' he asks. "We prolonged her misery for no more than a few brief days, for although Longoli did let her into his compound, he took her food and gave her neither food nor water. Even worse,'' continues Turnbull, "we reminded her of when things had been different, of days when children had cared for parents and parents for children. She was already dead,'' he concludes, "and we made her unhappy as well. At the time I was sure we were right,'' he states, "doing the only 'human' thing. In a way we *were*—we were making life more comfortable for ourselves, confirming our own sense of superiority. But now I wonder." Turnbull explains. "In the end I had a greater respect for the Ik, and I wonder if their way was not right, if I too should not have stood with the little crowd at the top of the *oror* and laughed as Lo'ono flapped about like a withered old tortoise on its back, then left her to die, perhaps laughing at herself, instead of crying." He describes the effect of his contemplation. "While I still fought hard to retain some of my old values and principles,'' he asserts, "others were simply washed away with Lo'ono's tears."[23]

Empathy for neglected, starving, and sickly old people and an initial conviction that his own values and attitudes were more humane than those of the Ik were responsible for Colin Turnbull's personal involvement in the lives of his chosen research subjects. For Hortense Powdermaker, however, boredom provided the motivation for subordinating professional concerns to personal participation in activities she had simply planned to observe and document. The events in question occurred while Powdermaker was studying the Lesu on the island of New Ireland in Melanesia.

A short time after her stay among the Lesu began, Powdermaker learned about plans for an initiation ceremony for eight adolescent boys. She welcomed the opportunity to witness such an event, for these rites, she knew, were held only when the number of initiates was sufficient to warrant the community preparation and participation required. Dancing by the women was an integral part of the festivities; Powdermaker was invited to attend the rehearsal sessions during which the women practiced the steps and movements that the male members of the society would be privy to observe only on the occasion of the initiation itself.

As she watched the women practice, night after night,

Powdermaker eventually became bored because of the repetitiveness of the rehearsals. She was asked to participate, but at first refused. "I was too self-conscious," she states. Instead, she "sat watching and held one of the babies." But "one evening," she reports, "I gathered my courage and began dancing." The vivacity of the dancers and the good-natured laughter that was evoked by her mistakes resulted in Powdermaker's becoming not only physically, but also emotionally, involved. Having taken the initial step, she continued to dance with the women night after night. "No longer were the evenings monotonous," she asserts.[24]

As the rehearsals continued and the time for the initiation approached, Powdermaker reports that she gave little thought to what she would do when the performance actually took place. She simply assumed that she would attend the ceremony, observe, and document the activities that marked the occasion. But the women had other expectations, and Powdermaker became aware of these when several of them presented her with decorative ornaments appropriate for dancers and asked her to wear a particular dress that was a favorite of theirs. Writes Powdermaker, "I gulped, and said I was not going to dance; I would just observe." But she realized that her involvement in the practice sessions was viewed as a commitment to participate in the public performance. "I could not explain that I had started because I was bored," she notes, "and that now I felt too self-conscious to participate in rites which I knew would be attended by thousands of natives from all over the island and nearby islands." Aware that her refusal to dance might offend or insult her hosts and teachers, Powdermaker felt she had no choice.[25]

As the initiation ceremony began, Powdermaker reflected on the scene. "Consumed with self-consciousness," she states, "I imagined my family and friends sitting in the background and muttering in disapproving tone, 'Hortense dancing with savages!'" The fact that her sister dancers and the members of the audience were natives and, in the eyes of some people, virtually living in the Stone Age, created what seemed to be an incongruous image. Hoping that an earthquake would disrupt the festivities, and fearing that she would collapse on her way to the performance area, Powdermaker nevertheless joined the others and began to dance.[26]

"Something happened," reports Powdermaker. "I forgot myself and was one with the dancers. Under the full moon and for the brief time of the dance, I ceased to be an anthropologist from a modern society. I danced." She further describes the outcome of her introspection. "I realized that, for this short period, I had been emotionally part of the rite," she states. "I was amused to realize that all the things white people had tried to make me fear—snakes, sharks, crocodiles, rape—had not caused me anxiety. Nor had the expedition [to Lesu] taken any particular courage," she continues. "But to dance with the women at the initiation rites—that had taken courage."[27]

The dancing over, Powdermaker reports that she reached for her notebook, assuming once again her role as investigator. She was invited to witness the actual circumcision of the eight adolescents, but chose not to do so. However, her participation in the dancing, and hence from her point of view in the initiation ceremony itself, had made her aware of the way in which personal involvement with subjects in terms of the shared identity of human being makes the distinction between fieldworker and subject of secondary importance, if not completely irrelevant, on specific occasions.[28]

The task of reconciling the tendency to relate to subjects in personal and human ways, and the motivation to maintain an impersonal, businesslike relationship with them is often complicated when fieldworkers befriend subjects (or vice versa). Attempting to subordinate rights and duties inherent in relationships between friends to those conceived as characteristic of fieldworker-subject interactions frequently creates dilemmas that lead to reflection and introspection. An experience of Hortense Powdermaker's among the Lesu is once again a case in point.

"My good friend Pulong was ill and no one knew whether she would live or die," Powdermaker writes. "In the early morning, before daybreak, she gave birth prematurely to her baby, born dead, and her own life appeared to be in danger. All day women of her clan were in her mother's house," she continues, "giving her native medicine, performing magic to cure, and tending her." Powdermaker describes her own reaction. "Psychologically, I was not at ease," she confesses. "I walked in and out of the house where Pulong lay, but I could do nothing. Obviously I knew too little of medicine to administer anything from my kit." But her lack of knowledge about illnesses and medications was not the principal source of her uneasiness. "Pulong was my best friend among the women and a very good informant," she asserts; "personal sorrow was mingled with fear of scientific loss. My sense of helplessness was difficult to take."[29]

Pulong's husband, Ongus, kept a vigil outside the house in which his ailing wife lay, forbidden by custom to be at her side because her illness was connected with childbirth. "Inanely I remarked to Ongus that I hoped Pulong would be better soon," she reports; "he replied gravely that he did not know. Even before he answered," she admits, "I knew my remark was silly."[30]

Powdermaker describes further what she did and how she felt. "I sat around the bed with the women, went back to my house, wrote up everything, wandered back to Pulong's bed again. The fact that I was getting good data did not take away my restlessness," she remarks. "I felt all wrong during this crisis: outside it, though emotionally involved." The dilemma she faced was only temporarily resolved with the outcome of this event. "Pulong recovered, the normal daily life was resumed and I lost this feeling," she states. "But during Pulong's illness and in similar emergencies," notes Powdermaker, "I knew that no matter how intimate and friendly I was with the natives, I was never truly a part of their lives." It was in terms of identities other than that of fellow human beings, however, that Powdermaker conceived the Lesu people and herself to differ.[31]

Powdermaker's friendship with Pulong developed over time. As it did, one can infer, the two women increasingly related to each other principally as friends, as is commonly and understandably the case with many fieldworkers and selected subjects. For with time and experience, relationships initiated to implement fieldwork plans often evolve from the impersonal to the personal, making strangers into friends. But sometimes individuals who are already friends assume the roles of fieldworker and subject, and the experience frequently makes them reflective and introspective, as Bruce Giuliano, Kathie O'Reilly, and Bari Polonsky discovered while carrying out a fieldwork project at UCLA.[32]

Motivated by an interest in the linguistic labels that Americans employ to identify each other, Giuliano, O'Reilly, and Polonsky generated a fieldwork plan that would enable them not only to elicit such terms, but also to determine the frequency of, and reasons for, their utilization. Drawing upon previous research which revealed that the labels people employ when speaking of Negroes, Italians, women, and homosexuals are often judged to be derogatory ("niggers," "wops," "broads," "queers," for example), the three researchers devised a time-limited, free-association "power test" to elicit from subjects other labels that come immediately to mind when they hear the words *Negro, Italian, woman,* and *homosexual.* The research design also called for interviews during which the fieldworkers could discuss the responses informally with the individual subjects, the intent being to elicit the subjects' own explanations for the linguistic labels they uttered in response to the stimulus words. Assuming that examples of, and reasons for, linguistic labeling could be obtained from any group of randomly-selected individuals, but also aware that the nature of the project might evoke suspicion or uneasiness from people who were strangers to them, the fieldworkers asked friends, who were also fellow graduate students of theirs at UCLA, to serve as research subjects.

Because of their friendships and shared student status, the fieldworkers and subjects initially anticipated no difficulties in implementing the project. They had all had previous fieldwork experience or knew enough about such research to interact objectively with each other. Following the completion of the word-association test, however, the three fieldworkers became reflective and introspective about the experience. In discussing their thoughts, they discovered that they had all experienced similar feelings of uneasiness. All realized that their efforts to behave as each felt a fieldworker should had made them uncomfortable. "We acted as though we believed, and we probably did in fact believe, that by reciting fixed formulae, under the right atmospheric conditions, like incantations, we could minimize our presence as human being," Giuliano, O'Reilly, and Polonsky state. "We imitated automata, assuming that any human response or reinforcement would infect the data, making it unscientific." But they discovered that their expectations were unrealistic. "In short," they assert, "we totally ignored the fact that in *any* interaction there is interaction, regardless of pretense."³³

The realizations that they did not—indeed, that no field-worker *can*—interact with subjects in a completely detached, impersonal manner led Giuliano, O'Reilly, and Polonsky to question their subjects individually, not only about their answers on the word-association test, but also about their reactions to, and assessments of, the experience. How had they felt about serving as subjects? Had they responded to the stimulus terms spontaneously and without forethought? Did they feel that their behavior had been affected by matters other than those relating directly to the word-association test?

These informal interviews, held outdoors rather than in the library conference room in which the word-association tests had been administered, were wide-ranging and informative. Some subjects admitted that they had rejected the first responses that came to mind when a stimulus term was uttered, searching instead for an alternative word that would be less likely to evoke negative reactions from fieldworkers who were also fellow students, friends, and human beings. Others reported that they had, indeed, responded spontaneously, sometimes regretting it after the fact, for they felt that the fieldworkers or others learning of their responses might judge them to be biased since the response words had pejorative connotations.

"We had assumed that the time necessary for evaluation would be nearly equivalent to the time necessary to enunciate that evaluation," state Giuliano, O'Reilly, and Polonsky. "We were wrong. Not having paused long enough to be aware of our thought processes," they continue, "we did not appreciate the incredible rapidity with which thought proceeds. We had failed to note," they add, "that in a space of time too brief to be measured or characterized, an individual may travel anywhere, and perhaps damn near everywhere, in the province of his life experience. We hadn't stopped to think that thinking never stops," they confess. "In those thirty seconds which we had imagined to be too brief for premeditation, many of our volunteers were led to relive years of agony . . . and we don't feel too good about ourselves."³⁴

Giuliano, O'Reilly, and Polonsky relate what it was they

learned from their fieldwork project about individuals' awareness of linguistic labeling.

> Our volunteers were aware that they formed opinions of themselves on the basis of their use of language, that they judged others on the basis of their use of language, and that they in turn were evaluated by others on the same basis. Therefore, they often consciously and carefully selected the words which were to make up their conversation, i.e., they often consciously chose between and among the words and phrases which were "available" to them. They were aware that words acted as a clue to who they were and how they wished to be perceived. By their words they also gave clues to how they perceived others, and to the nature of the relationship which they wished to establish with them.
>
> On the other hand, there were times when our volunteers wished to signal that their language was not to be taken as a clue to who they were, or of the relationships which they wished to establish with us. In such cases, the negative feelings that an individual had toward a word, on the basis of his prior experiences, might be defeated [i.e., subordinated or suppressed] by his perception of sufficient reason for uttering it.[35]

What else did their fieldwork experience reveal? Giuliano, O'Reilly, and Polonsky learned that their subjects "were constantly aware of their actual audience"—that is, of the three individuals who administered the word-association test and conducted the interviews. Moreover, the three fieldworkers discovered during the interviews that the ways in which their subjects identified them (as fellow graduate students, friends, human beings, a male and two females, for instance) frequently played a part in determining the subjects' responses to the stimulus terms and the subjects' reactions to their own responses when these were actually uttered without conscious forethought.[36]

Finally, note Giuliano, O'Reilly, and Polonsky, the subjects' comments during the interviews revealed that "they were constantly aware, if not wary, of a potential audience, in the form of people who might eventually hear the things which they were

saying." The subjects knew in advance that the word-association test and the interviews were being tape recorded and that
the results of the fieldwork project would be made known to
others. This awareness also played a part in determining the
nature of some of the answers the subjects gave on the test and,
more importantly, in evoking the reflection and introspection
that evolved as the subjects pondered their responses in retrospect and contemplated the ways in which others might interpret and react to them.[37]

As the Giuliano-O'Reilly-Polonsky project demonstrates,
those who are cast in the subject role, like those who function as
fieldworkers, often become reflective and introspective. As is
the case with fieldworkers, subjects frequently feel uneasy
about being so identified. Furthermore, being queried about
their own and others' behaviors, and having their answers and
actions documented in writing, on magnetic tape, or on film,
can understandably raise questions in their minds about the
fieldworker-subject relationship and its implications. Unfortunately, individuals who serve as research subjects seldom have
the opportunity to reveal in print their reactions to, and assessments of, their experiences *as subjects.* But published remarks
that fieldworkers make about their experiences with specific
subjects suggest that reflection and introspection are as common among subjects as they are among fieldworkers.

One complaint sometimes registered by fieldworkers is that
individuals who initially serve willingly as informants later
become indifferent or uncooperative, as evidenced by their failure to appear for prearranged appointments or their refusal to
continue to respond to the fieldworker's questions. In the diary
he kept while conducting fieldwork among the Northwest
Pacific Coast Indians, Franz Boas reports several such instances. One involved a Tsimsian whom Boas identifies initially
as "my friend Mathew" but who became a frequent "no-show"
for scheduled meetings. Another involved an anonymous old
woman (also Tsimsian) who pleased Boas by willingly telling
him lengthy stories on their first meeting, but who refused to tell
him anything subsequently.

Boas's reaction in both cases was one of anger. "I am cross
because my Tsimsian has deserted me," he writes of Mathew in
his diary entry of September 24, 1886. "From experience I
should know that such things happen," he continues, "but it is

easier said than done not to be angry about it." Recording his reaction was not the end of the matter, however. Boas also made Mathew aware of his feelings. "I told the good man who, by the way, is one of the most religious," he reveals, "that he was the greatest liar I had ever known since he did not keep his word. I told him I would tell his pastor about it."[38]

From Boas's point of view, Mathew and the old Tsimsian woman were simply uncooperative. Their failure to comply with his requests for information, he concludes, was due to their irresponsibility or unreliability. He does not consider the possibility that the two may have felt uneasy about being identified as subjects or that they may have had specific reasons for not wishing to work further with him or to divulge additional information to him following their initial encounters with him. That Boas admits to being angry because of this change in relationships suggests that his explanation for the "noncooperation" of the two Tsimsians may have been a manifestation of his emotional state. That they were communicative at first but reticent later suggests that if the two "uncooperative Indians" could have been queried and persuaded to answer honestly, they might have given entirely different reasons for their unwillingness to tell tribal stories and answer other questions about their way of life for a man who was a stranger in their midst.

Another clue that serving as subjects makes some individuals reflective, and that their reflection may have results that fieldworkers do not anticipate, is provided by reported instances in which subjects are known to have duped, exploited, misinformed, or misled fieldworkers, sometimes deliberately and sometimes inadvertently. Among those who describe such experiences in print are Robert Lowie, Franz Boas, Napoleon Chagnon, Herbert Gans, and Edward Norbeck.

While studying a group of Plains Indians, Robert Lowie discovered that a fieldworker can be unexpectedly exploited by subjects. The occasion was a social dance which he attended with his interpreter. He noticed that much time passed after everyone had convened, but that nobody danced. Finally, a woman approached a drummer, who began to play. She then tugged at Lowie's blanket, a gesture indicative of her desire to have him dance with her. He refused to acknowledge the request at first, but eventually yielded. He describes what happened. "To my delight," he reports, "the squaw who did my laundering invited me and the two of us shuffled along with the rest. When the drummers stopped, the couples broke up," he continues, "and to my surprise my washer-woman opened a beaded purse and handed me a dime; my interpreter, I discovered, was getting only a nickel from *his* partner." But Lowie's initial pleasure at his seeming worth was short lived. "However, my lady's generosity was not motivated by my personal charms," he admits. "As my interpreter explained, it was my duty to invite her at the next dance and to pay her twice the amount received from her. In other words," Lowie explains, "she had contrived a safe one-hundred per cent investment." But that was not the end of the matter. "However, not content, she returned to the charge at the third dance, bringing a chum with her," he notes, "so that I had to circle about with both women, an arm around each one's shoulders." The consequences were clear. "I got two fees for my efforts and was duty bound to double them in my final performance that night," he reports. Whether intended as a practical joke or as a means of underscoring the differences in financial well-being between him and his subjects, the experience left Lowie with the feeling that he had been exploited, a feeling that might have been intensified in part by the fact that Lowie did not speak or understand the native language of his subjects.[39]

Lack of proficiency in the language of one's subjects was also the basis for Franz Boas's once having been duped by an American Indian informant. "A Comox woman narrated to me for two hours in Comox," Boas reports in his diary entry for November 18, 1886, "and I thought I had obtained a nice text." But he felt a bit uneasy as he was recording the woman's words. "While I was writing I wondered why there was so little narrative, only questions and answers," he states, "but this often occurs in tales and I did not worry much about it." His suspicions were confirmed later, however. "But it turned out to be a made-up conversation: 'How are you? Shall we go and look for berries? No, I do not feel like it, etc.'" Boas does not describe his reaction, but the next three sentences in the diary entry suggest that he did not let the matter pass without comment. "Well, maybe now I shall get a text," the entry continues. "They tried yesterday to raise their price, but I did not agree. Fortunately they are nice enough not to cause any unpleasantness." The promise of remuneration for telling tales to a fieldworker who was not proficient in the language may have played a part in motivating the Comox woman to dupe Boas by making up a conversation that he could not initially distinguish from the telling of a tribal tale.[40]

While Boas apparently realized that he had been duped shortly after the act had been committed, and Lowie felt that he was being exploited while it was happening, fieldworkers frequently learn much later (and sometimes, no doubt, they never do discover) that subjects have given them inaccurate information. The extent of the deception and the reasons for it are often complex, as Napoleon Chagnon found out from several experiences with the Yanomamö Indians of Venezuela.

"With respect to collecting the data I sought," writes Chagnon, "there was a very frustrating problem. Primitive social organization is kinship organization," he explains, "and to understand the Yanomamö way of life I had to collect extensive genealogies." But the task, he admits, was not an easy one. "I could not have deliberately picked a more difficult group to work with in this regard," he notes, adding, "They have very stringent name taboos. They attempt to name people in such a way that when the person dies and they can no longer use his name," he continues, "the loss of the word in the language is not inconvenient." Chagnon exemplifies the practice. "Hence, they name people for specific and minute parts of things, such as 'toenail of some rodent,' thereby being able to retain the words 'toenail' and '(specific) rodent,' but not being able to refer directly to the toenail of that rodent." He elaborates further. "The taboo is maintained even for the living: One mark of prestige is the courtesy others show you by not using your name." He speculates about the reason for this. "The sanctions behind the taboo seem to be an unusual combination of fear and respect."[41]

In continuing, Chagnon explains why the name taboo adversely affected his genealogical research. "I tried to use kinship terms to collect genealogies at first," he reports, "but the kinship terms were so ambiguous that I ultimately had to resort to names." The Yanomamö response was reactionary. "They were quick to grasp that I was bound to learn everybody's name and reacted, without my knowing it, by inventing false names for everybody in the village," states Chagnon. "After having spent several months collecting names and learning them," he reveals, "this came as a disappointment to me: I could not cross-check the genealogies with other informants from distant villages."[42]

Chagnon reports the reaction of the Yanomamö. "They enjoyed watching me learn these names," he asserts. "I assumed, wrongly, that I would get the truth to each question and that I would get the best information by working in public." But his assumption proved incorrect. "This set the stage for converting a serious project into a farce," he notes. "Each informant tried to outdo his peers by inventing a name even more ridiculous than what I had been given earlier, or by asserting that the individual about whom I inquired was married to his mother or daughter, and the like." He describes the tactic he employed. "I would have the informant whisper the name of the individual in my ear, noting that he was the father of such and such a child. Everybody would then insist that I repeat the name aloud," he continues, "roaring in hysterics as I clumsily pronounced the name." Chagnon offers his interpretation of the laughter. "I assumed that the laughter was in response to the violation of the name taboo or to my pronunciation," he confesses, adding, "This was a reasonable interpretation, since the individual whose name I said aloud invariably became angry." Once again, however, he discovered that his assumption was erroneous. "After I learned what some of the names meant," he reports, "I began to understand what the laughter was all about. A few of the more colorful examples are: 'hairy vagina,' 'long penis,' 'feces of the harpy eagle,' and 'dirty rectum.' No wonder the victims were angry." Chagnon concludes.[43]

Once he realized that he had been deliberately misinformed and he understood the reasons why, Chagnon devised an alternative means of eliciting genealogical information. He met with subjects singly and in private, and in this way he began to get the same names for specific individuals from different informants, suggesting that the Yanomamö were at last being cooperative and honest. "Little by little I extended the genealogies and learned real names," he indicates. Yet while he was eventually given the correct names of living Yanomamö, Chagnon discovered that he was deceived by the responses he got about the names of the dead. "Most of them gave me the name of a living man as the father of some individual in order to avoid mentioning that the actual father was dead," he notes.[44]

"The quality of a genealogy depends in part on the number of generations it embraces, and the name taboo prevented me from getting any substantial information about deceased ancestors," Chagnon explains. "Without this information," he continues, "I could not detect marriage patterns through time." Moreover, to get such information, he "had to rely on older informants," and, he reports, "these were the most reluctant of all. As I became more proficient in the language and more skilled at detecting lies," writes Chagnon, "my informants became better at lying. One of them in particular was so cunning and persuasive that I was shocked to discover that he had been inventing information." He explains. "He specialized in making a ceremony out of telling me false names," notes Chagnon. "He would look around to make sure nobody was listening outside my hut, enjoin me to never mention the name again, act very nervous and spooky, and then grab me by the head to whisper the name very softly into my ear." Chagnon describes his response. "I was always elated after an informant session with him," he writes, "because I had several generations of dead ancestors for the living people. The others refused to give me this information." Chagnon's delight motivated him to reward his cooperative informant. "To show my gratitude," he states, "I paid him quadruple the rate I had given the others. When word got around that I had increased the pay, volunteers began pouring in to give me genealogies."[45]

The man whom Chagnon rewarded for his willingness to divulge genealogical secrets, as it turned out, had deliberately lied, and the discovery of this fact was made quite by accident. A dispute broke out in the village "over the possession of a woman." As it intensified, one of the combatants called an adversary by the name of the man's dead father. "I quickly seized on this as an opportunity to collect an accurate genealogy," writes Chagnon, "and pumped him about his adversary's ancestors." In his angry state, the young man provided the requested information, which conflicted with that presented by the elderly "cooperative informant." Notes Chagnon, "I challenged his information, and he explained that everybody knew that the old man was deceiving me and bragging about it in the village." Chagnon explains what else he was told. "The names the old man had given me were the dead ancestors of the members of a village so far away that he thought I would never have occasion to inquire about them.'' But the information provided by the young man who had been involved in the dispute proved to be accurate, requiring Chagnon to reexamine and reevaluate the genealogical data he had been accumulating. ''Thus, after five months of almost constant work on the genealogies of just one group,'' he reports, ''I had to begin almost from scratch!''[46]

As was the case for Napoleon Chagnon, Herbert Gans discovered that obtaining accurate information about a sensitive subject made one of his fieldwork projects a source of reflection and introspection. The phenomenon into which Gans wished to inquire was politics rather than genealogies, and the setting was a suburb of a large American city instead of a small-scale tribal society that existed in an environment alien to the fieldworker. But the problems Gans and Chagnon faced in trying to elicit information and in attempting to determine the accuracy of the information provided were strikingly similar.

''Actually, the most difficult research problem was untangling political events,'' writes Gans. ''I could not always get honest responses from some politicians; even when I did,'' he notes, ''they saw things so much from their own perspective that I was always faced with the problem of reconciling conflicting accounts.'' He elaborates, explaining why responses to questions about political events were more difficult to obtain than were answers to queries about other aspects of life in Levittown. ''The difficulty was not so much in finding out *what* happened as *why*,'' he asserts. ''Political strategies are very complex even in a small community, the motivations that create these strategies are often unfathomable, and politicians are not always willing (or able) to reveal their motives and goals.'' Gans suggests means of resolving this dilemma. ''One solution is to talk to their opponents, ask them to explain an action, and then confront the original actor with the explanation.'' He characterizes the likely effect. ''Usually this produces denials, but sometimes it results in more detailed explanations than would otherwise be given, and these can then be checked out with others. Another solution,'' he continues, ''is to find a trustworthy person who is marginal to the group being studied and depend on him for final verification. Such people are rare, however,'' explains Gans, ''for if one is involved in politics it is difficult to remain marginal.'' But he had good luck. ''I was fortunate in being able to find a couple of marginal people, as well as a local newspaperman who was 'in the know' but sufficiently detached from the political process to serve as an informant,'' he reveals. ''When these sources were not available, I had to rely on the information given me by people whom I trusted, and while this may have introduced some bias into the data, because I was more likely to trust people I liked and those of my own educational background, I had no other alternative. Sometimes,'' Gans concludes, ''what really happens in politics is virtually unknowable to an outsider, and the only solution is for the researcher to become a participant and keep notes in the process.''[47]

In this passage, quoted from his well-known study of a suburban American community, Gans illustrates that a fieldworker often becomes uneasy, and perhaps even concerned, about the quantity and quality of information that subjects sometimes provide. Moreover, he offers several reasons for subjects' reticence or for their presenting the fieldworker with information of questionable validity. Some behaviors, Gans contends, are so complex that individuals cannot discuss or explain them, and even when they can do so, many people prefer to withhold information because of their fear that providing it might ''reveal their motives and goals.'' Not noted by Gans is the fact that subjects speak from experience, that experiences obviously differ, and that the very process of answering questions in terms of one's experiences may lead one to distort or idealize events or behaviors, as Edward Norbeck and his wife discovered while conducting fieldwork in Japan.

''My wife, who does not speak Japanese, also recorded notes in shorthand, typing them later,'' Norbeck reports. ''Making use of a Japanese woman from Okayama City as an interpreter,'' he adds, ''she gathered information from Takashima women on child-rearing and other 'women's affairs.''' He explains the results. ''We both found it necessary to verify carefully the information given by our informants, mostly because no two informants had quite the same experiences or views of the world.'' Norbeck exemplifies this point. ''One aged informant described in detail an annual cycle of religious events that required many sheets of paper for typing—and, it turned out, included ceremonies observed during the informant's youth but now long obsolete.'' He provides another and somewhat different instance. ''A middle-aged woman who had known only poverty and unremitting work declared, honestly enough from her own viewpoint, that the annual ceremonial calendar consisted of two events falling on two days of the year when she was able to rest and feel festive." Norbeck notes further, in continuing, that the tendency to idealize, as well as the necessity to draw upon idiosyncratic experiences and views, also played its part. "Some informants reported only ideal standards of behavior, as our attempts to verify their statements sometimes brought out." Once again, he provides an illustration. "During one of the annual festivals when 'all' people were said to visit the small Shinto shrine in the community, I kept a continual watch on the shrine and found the visitors totaled eleven people, young children accompanied by aged grandmothers."[48]

The Norbecks' awareness that their information needed to be critically assessed developed not only from their discernment of inconsistencies in different subjects' responses to the same questions, but also from suspicions aroused and subsequently confirmed because of the behavior of the woman who served as Ms. Norbeck's interpreter. "By observation of gestures and other nonverbal forms of communication," Edward Norbeck relates, "my wife noted that her otherwise excellent interpreter omitted or altered to greater elegance any account of custom, such as some of the local practices of toilet training and weaning, that she as an educated woman raised in Tokyo thought barbaric." He explains what this discovery necessitated. "Much checking and rechecking of these subjects and others were done by use of multiple informants and observation," he reports. "Some of the information supplied by my wife's interpreter had to be changed on the basis of interviews I later conducted."[49]

The Norbecks' experiences, together with those of the other individuals characterized in this chapter, suggest some of the many sources and reasons for reflection and introspection that occur when individuals are cast in either the fieldworker or subject role. Those whose fieldwork experiences expose them to ways of living and thinking that differ from those to which they are accustomed often become reflective and introspective as they discern and contemplate the contrasts. Furthermore, both fieldworkers and subjects understandably behave and assess each others' behavior in accordance with their conceptions of the motives, purposes, and implications of their interactions. Subject and fieldworker both ponder the same kinds of questions: Who is this individual? Why does she or he behave as she or he does? Can I believe what she or he tells me? How involved can or should I allow myself to become with him or her? How do we differ, how are we similar, and why? Such questions are ones that arise in the minds of human beings, whoever they are and whenever and wherever they happen to encounter each other. That attempting to generate answers to them is an integral aspect of the experience of fieldwork should therefore come as no surprise.

Results

F rom the moment individuals first contemplate fieldwork, they consider also the probable results of their
efforts. As was noted in earlier chapters of this book,
fieldwork is a purposive act in which people engage to achieve
predetermined ends. The principal objective for doing fieldwork may be to fulfill a requirement for a class, to generate
data that can serve as the basis for a thesis or dissertation, to
satisfy a prerequisite for admission to certain disciplinary-based
communities of scholars, to enhance relative social or professional status, to gain or maintain peer or public recognition, or
to obtain financial reward. Rarely, if ever, do individuals plan
and implement fieldwork projects solely because of self-stimu-
lation or for self-satisfaction, and never do they do so only
because of dedication or commitment to inquiry, despite frequent claims that this is the case. Because there are always personal motives for undertaking fieldwork, there is, from the
beginning, always a concern with results.

When employed in discussions of fieldwork, the word *results*
usually has as its referent some specific final product, such as a
written report, a published essay, a book, a sound recording, a
film, a photographic display, or an exhibit of artifacts. Many
fieldwork projects, of course, have one or some combination of
such phenomena as their outputs, and fieldworkers usually
aspire to produce some tangible evidence of the results of their
labors, even though the end-product envisioned may never actu-

ally materialize. But the results of fieldwork entail more than
the objects produced and presented to others to document and
describe in retrospect an individual's completed fieldwork
adventure. Like the confrontations considered in chapter three,
the clarifications and compromises discussed in chapter four,
and the reflection and introspection illustrated in chapter five,
the results of fieldwork are continuous and ongoing. They are
in evidence both during and following the period of encounter
between fieldworkers and subjects, and both before and after
any tangible outputs of the fieldwork experience have been
created and disseminated. Since they evolve from interactions
between people studying people at first hand, the results of
fieldwork include more than the discrete phenomena that con-
vey findings and supporting data to an audience of other people.

There is justification for defining *results* more broadly than is
customary in discussions of fieldwork. The results of fieldwork
include the intangible and human as well as the tangible and
impersonal; they are characteristically ongoing, diverse, complex, and often unpredictable. For example, the fieldwork for
the Festinger-Riecken-Schachter book, *When Prophecy Fails*
(see chapter 4), demonstrates how observing and documenting a
short-lived event can lead to decisions and actions that may
result inadvertently in the reinforcement of convictions and the
perpetuation of behaviors that might otherwise not persist. Jean
Briggs's relationships with her principal Utkuhlikhalingmiut
Eskimo informant, Inuttiaq (see chapter 4) indicates that when
fieldworkers and subjects have different sets of expectations
about their rights and responsibilities vis-à-vis each other, conflicts may result, creating tensions that can only be alleviated if
the parties involved are willing and able to clarify and compromise. Colin Turnbull's reactions to the younger Ik's treatment
of their ailing and starving elders (see chapter 5) illustrates that
a fieldworker's adherence to values and standards of behavior
that contrast with those of selected subjects can produce as well
as solve problems, with the problems produced sometimes being
of greater consequence than those that are solved. Such effects
of fieldwork experiences upon the human beings involved are to
be counted among the results of fieldwork, though they are
rarely conceived or discussed as such, despite the fact that they
are often the bases for the most significant learning that occurs.

While many of the effects of fieldwork upon the individuals

involved are neither predictable nor brought about through conscious efforts, some effects are produced by fieldworkers' deliberate employment of strategies to accomplish preplanned objectives. Since fieldworkers are preoccupied with gathering information or data, they most often employ such strategies to obtain from subjects the specific kinds of information they desire. That this determination to achieve results—in the form of data—can produce results—in the form of effects upon the human beings concerned—is apparent from the fieldwork experiences of innumerable individuals, including those of Jerry Hyman.

While a graduate student in anthropology at the University of Chicago, Jerry Hyman became interested in the potlatch as practiced by the Northwest Pacific Coast Indians. Aware of this ceremonial giving away of goods from the writings of such earlier fieldworkers as Franz Boas, Hyman decided to make it his first fieldwork project. "I wanted to know what had happened to the old potlatch," he writes, and he wished to do so, he adds, "by my own particular empirical encounter with a real, live potlatch."[1]

Having spent a summer on the island of Taku in southeastern Alaska, Hyman had become acquainted with some of the Indian inhabitants of the area. The Tlingit family with whom he had stayed on his initial visit had invited him to return. Knowing that there were two large community, as well as several small family, potlatches scheduled for the summer of 1967, Hyman accepted the invitation of David and Sarah, his Indian hosts. He regarded them as friends who could serve as his intermediaries with the larger population, interceding on his behalf to ensure him an invitation to the ceremonies. The expected invitation was never issued, however, for despite the attempts by David and Sarah to persuade members of the community to allow their house guest to attend the potlatches, permission was denied.

Hyman viewed the decision to exclude him as indicative of more than merely Indian inhospitality. "People were starting to 'be against me,'" he states, adding, "I had visions of being expelled." But he was determined "to counter the growing, hardening opposition." So he developed a strategy that would ensure his safety and enable him to remain on the island during the time the ceremonies were held. This strategy, Hyman acknowledges, entailed a series of moves designed to put pressure on his Tlingit hosts, making it difficult, if not impossible, for them to accede to the demands of community leaders that Hyman be excluded from all the ceremonies (including David and Sarah's own family potlatch) and that he perhaps even be asked to leave Taku.[2]

The basis for Hyman's evolving plan of action was economic. David and Sarah, he reports, "were relatively poor," and "they needed money for their own party." Hyman realized that he "represented, through a 'generous' estimation of room and board costs, an income they could now (more than ever) ill-afford to lose." So he "impressed this upon them," aware, he notes, that "If I needed them, they also needed me." Furthermore, his desire to carry out his project and to get results (in the form of information obtained through firsthand observation) seemed to him to justify such a strategy. "I had come to study potlatch," he writes. "I felt I had to see one." He could do nothing about the decision to bar him from the two large community ceremonies. "But," he asserts, "there was the third party, admittedly (because of its relative humility) treated in the village as something of an afterthought, but no less on that account a real party from the anthropological perspective." This was the potlatch to be given by David and Sarah. "And over this party," notes Hyman, "given by 'my own family,' I had at least some leverage. I moved calculatedly and cautiously to actualize it," he continues, revealing why doing so was important to him. "The potential prize was a firsthand look at a potlatch and the attendant academic success. The potential cost was academic and personal failure, expulsion from the village, and return to Chicago as an ethnographic washout."[3]

In continuing, Hyman describes the specifics of his strategy. "I began simply asserting in the house, in off-hand, indirect sorts of ways, my acceptance of the already tendered invitation." He exemplifies his actions. "I would say things like 'When our party comes . . . ,' 'I can't wait to . . . ,' 'Will I be sitting with . . .' All very indirect and periodic, with intervals calculated to be long enough so that the family would feel unjustified in becoming angry but short enough to keep my continued participation the foregone conclusion I labored to make it seem." He even "sat at the kitchen table where the family planning took place even though I couldn't understand the half-

Tlingit, half-English in which it was discussed.'' Furthermore, he ''used one boy, an orphan whom David and Sarah were paid to raise, as a kind of 'spy' within the household: he would translate from the Tlingit conversations they may not have wanted me to understand,'' notes Hyman, adding, ''I kept the pot simmering.''[4]

Hyman's plan seemed to be working. But one night ''a meeting of all the families giving parties'' was called. Hyman was ''of course, excluded.'' So he ''went to bed early,'' though he also ''stayed awake.'' When David and Sarah returned, Hyman overheard them talking at the kitchen table. ''I could tell by the tone,'' he writes, ''that things had not gone well.'' So, he reports, ''I planned what I would do.''[5]

The next morning, Hyman learned that a decision had been made to exclude him from the family, as well as the community, potlatches. Sarah broke the news. '' 'I don't understand it,' '' Hyman quotes Sarah as having said. '' 'How the people are against you, Jerry. I don't understand it. I have never seen anything like it.' '' It was obvious to Hyman that the pressure on David and Sarah from other Tlingits was greater than that he had himself applied. But that was not to be the end of the matter.[6]

''I played it cool,'' Hyman states in reporting what happened next. ''I certainly didn't want them to do anything which would get them into trouble, I said, and if that meant I couldn't go to the party, then I couldn't go.'' Instead, he told David and Sarah, he ''would just have to talk to them about it.'' But he admits that what he said and what he meant were not the same thing.[7]

The new developments motivated Hyman to employ new tactics. He bought a case of soft drinks at the local grocery store and ''asked that they be delivered to David and Sarah's,'' fully aware that they ''would know who had sent the drinks probably before they even arrived at the house.'' Hyman ''also knew what the drinks meant.'' He explains: ''Drinks were the kinds of things kinsmen and only kinsmen were expected to donate to a party. They constitute elements of hospitality at the party and are therefore appropriate only for kinsmen to contribute.'' Hence, his generous gesture had obvious implications. ''Their acceptance of the drinks, a symbol of kinship, was tantamount to the creation of a fictive kinship relationship between us,'' he writes. "It was of course possible for them to refuse the gift," Hyman remarks, "but given their financial position and the social strain of refusing, I guessed they wouldn't." His guess proved correct, for David and Sarah accepted the gift and, as Hyman anticipated, the couple was forced "to buck village pressure" and to invite him, as their kinsman, to their family potlatch.[8]

That the community leaders were as determined to exclude Hyman as he was to be included became obvious when another meeting was called two nights before David and Sarah's potlatch was to take place. The results were the same as those of the earlier meeting, and Sarah apologetically informed Hyman once again that he would not be permitted to attend the family's ceremony. Since he could think of no additional tactic to employ, Hyman conceived himself to be defeated. "I again tried to secure assurance of at least a secondhand description," he reports. "I would have to settle for that. There was nothing to do but retreat gracefully and wait the party out." But an unexpected development provided Hyman with yet another opportunity to secure an invitation. As Sarah and her sister were preparing the food on the day before their potlatch, they discovered that they did not have enough meat. "They would need more. Where could they get another deer?" Someone remarked that a matrilineal cousin had recently shot a deer, but when asked to contribute it, he insisted on a payment of twenty dollars. Such a response was unheard of, but attempts to negotiate failed. "The cousin was adamant. He demanded the $20. The family decided to refuse," Hyman states. "They would not pay a kinsman for what was rightfully theirs. Still they were deerless and were therefore about to be seriously embarrassed."[9]

Hyman recognized the opportunity to help as his "final chance" to be a witness to the potlatch. "I waited 'till the whole thing had been settled in the early evening," he reports. "It was too late for any more village meetings. I told Sarah I knew a teacher who had just come back from a hunting trip with some deer," he continues. "I volunteered to see if I could get one. I told them to let me know the following morning whether they wanted me to do so." No decision had been made by morning; but as the day progressed and the time necessary to prepare and cook the deer lapsed, David and Sarah accepted Hyman's offer. He obtained a deer from the teacher, paying twenty dollars for it. "Not only had I defined myself as a nuclear kinsman earlier," writes Hyman, "I had now come through as a kinsman when 'real' kinsmen had failed them. I would not of course accept payment," he continues, adding, "They were stuck." But, Hyman insists, "At least they had a handle against the community pressure. No one could deny their obligation to invite me." The results were predictable. "That night I attended my first and only party," notes Hyman. "I therefore became, by definition, a Tlingit. I left Taku the same week."[10]

Hyman got the results he desired. His strategy had won him an invitation to the kind of ceremony he had decided to study, and the invitation enabled him to obtain the information he had wanted in the way he wished to get it—by his "own particular empirical encounter with a real, live potlatch." But these results, in the form of data, created results, in the form of effects upon the human beings involved. It is apparent from Hyman's account of his experience that the effects upon people of tactics employed to gain access to information are not always unplanned or unexpected. Sometimes these effects are brought about by systematic strategies designed to evoke predictable responses from selected subjects, thereby creating opportunities for fieldworkers to accomplish their research objectives.

Hyman's experience illustrates one way in which fieldworkers can be said to manipulate their subjects in order to get desired results in the form of data. Another commonly-employed technique entails fieldworkers' providing, through their own behavior or that of willing accomplices, preplanned stimuli intended to evoke the kinds of behavior or events the fieldworker wishes to witness. To stimulate subjects to tell stories or sing songs, for example, fieldworkers sometimes first narrate or sing themselves, hoping that subjects will respond in kind so that the fieldworker can document their behavior when they assume the storyteller's or singer's role. Richard M. Dorson and Kenneth S. Goldstein, among others, advocate such a tactic as a useful means of motivating subjects to narrate or to sing and hence as a technique that can facilitate a fieldworker's collecting stories or songs for subsequent study.[11] Promising and providing remuneration to subjects for specific kinds of information are also often used as stimuli to enable fieldworkers to get desired results. As was noted in the preceding chapter, Napoleon Chagnon employed this technique to obtain carefully-guarded genealogical information from the Yanomamö Indians; and one result was that when it became generally known that he was paying well for genealogies of their dead ancestors, the Yanomamö were eager to comply with Chagnon's request, supplying him willingly with information that he learned only later was erroneous. Offering subjects such other things as alcoholic beverages, tobacco, and inexpensive trinkets to motivate them to divulge information or to reward them for having done so is another practice frequently utilized and recommended by fieldworkers to facilitate the task of obtaining the kinds of information they wish.[12] While it is sometimes argued that compensating subjects for their cooperation is only fair and often beneficial to them, it is also obvious that when such techniques are deliberately used as means to accomplish predetermined ends, the effects of these acts, as well as the information obtained by engaging in them, constitute results of fieldwork.

Enlisting members of the research population, or individuals well known to selected subjects, to serve as accomplices to fieldworkers is also often proposed as a potentially effective means of getting the desired information, and hence the results. Kenneth S. Goldstein regards this as a technique for "inducting natural context." By having the accomplice behave in a way that is likely to stimulate some subject(s) to exhibit behavior or provide information the fieldworker wants to observe or record, he indicates, the subjects' behavior, though induced, still "occurs naturally" and in the kind of "social context" in which it is commonly and appropriately in evidence.[13] Goldstein reports that he once used his daughter as an accomplice to stimulate other children to play marbles with her in her yard, enabling her father to observe and take notes on the activity as he sat nearby purportedly writing letters.[14] On another occasion, his accomplice was a young Scots woman whose task was to get one of her aunts to tell a particular story in the presence of a second aunt (the narrator's sister) so that Goldstein could record the telling on tape and subsequently elicit the story and record it again, this time from each of the two women. His goal was to determine the degree of consistency between the first aunt's two tellings of the same tale, on the one hand, and to discover the extent to which the first aunt's telling might have caused the second aunt to modify her version of the story after she had heard her sister present her own somewhat different version, on the other.[15] One result of these experiments was that Goldstein got the information he desired. Because the subjects were apparently never told that an experiment had been conducted, that they were involved in it, and that the observation and documentation of their behavior were the goals of the experiment, another obvious result was that the subjects were manipulated to enable the fieldworker not only to get information, but also to obtain it more "naturally" than he felt would have been possible by such other means as interviewing.

Often coupled with the fieldworker's desire to get results in the form of information of specific kinds is the wish to record information in particular ways. Unlike their nineteenth and early twentieth-century predecessors, who had to rely solely on their memories and handwritten notes as records of, and bases for reconstructing, their fieldwork ventures, contemporary fieldworkers have at their disposal sophisticated equipment that enables them to document mechanically much of what they see and hear. Magnetic tape and film can capture aspects of behavior that fieldworkers often do not even perceive initially and that they frequently cannot remember or represent adequately (if at all) in writing. Yet while tape recorders and cameras can facilitate the fieldworker's information-gathering tasks and provide the potential for more thorough descriptions and analyses because of the comprehensiveness and permanency of the records they produce, utilizing such devices can have other results as well.

A fieldworker's desire to record information or document behavior on magnetic tape or film inevitably introduces additional complexities into an already complex human situation. Making mental or written records of what people say and do causes some amount of uneasiness in both the sources and the recordmakers. When subjects know or suspect that their behavior is under scrutiny, there is, understandably, a tendency for them to be guarded in what they say and more conscious than usual of what they do. Similarly, observing or querying subjects and making mental or written notes for future reference make many fieldworkers feel somewhat intrusive. But their awareness of the limitations of the human memory and of the selectivity of notetaking enables most individuals to live with whatever uneasiness might develop. When their interaction extends over time, any uneasiness tends to be reduced or alleviated, for both fieldworkers and subjects realize that with the passage of time, much that is observed and communicated will be forgotten, overlooked, or reinterpreted in light of the developing relationships between them. The introduction of a tape recorder or camera complicates matters, however, for many individuals feel that such devices, being nonhuman, are less selective and more inclusive than the humans who operate them, and that the records these machines produce, being permanent and reproducible, can be made available to wider audiences. A fieldworker's desire to use a tape recorder or camera (or both) thus raises some significant questions. Should such devices be used at all in fieldwork involving people studying people at first hand? If so, should they be employed openly or surreptitiously? If they are utilized openly, then how should one introduce them? Should the fieldworker ask subjects for permission to tape or film what they say or do? What explanation or justification should the fieldworker offer for wanting to tape or film? What effects might one's using a tape recorder or camera have upon subjects' behaviors or the information they present? Finally, what does the fieldworker do if subjects refuse to allow filming or taping?

Such questions have no simple or single answers. Knowing this, some fieldworkers avoid confronting the issues involved and decide not to use mechanical recording devices at all. Instead, they choose to rely upon their memories and note-taking, recording their recollections and elaborating upon their notes when they are away from subjects and can document their experiences more extensively in writing or on tape. Such a choice may result in records of lesser quantity and quality. Another result is that the fieldworker may avoid one possible basis for alienating or arousing suspicions in her or his subjects.

While the decision not to tape or film is always an option, the accessibility and efficiency of mechanical recording devices increase the pressures on fieldworkers to make use of these technological inventions. Remembering and note-taking are taxing experiences, and individuals who rely exclusively upon memory and notes always stand the chance of being charged with incompleteness or bias. Documenting behavior on tape or film frees the fieldworker, to some extent, from the tasks of trying not to forget and of writing when one could perhaps learn more from watching. And sound recordings and photographic records, being perceptible to others, are often regarded as a definitive means of justifying, exemplifying, and attesting to the accuracy of descriptions and analyses fieldworkers present in public forums and in print. Hence, the tape recorder and camera have come increasingly to be regarded as standard and essential pieces of equipment for the fieldworker. The desire or unstated requirement that audible and visual records be among the results of fieldwork sometimes results in decisions, actions, and frustrations of considerable consequence.

An experience of Mary Anne Chapman's is a case in point. To fulfill a requirement for a graduate course in fieldwork, Chapman proposed and carried out a project to determine why makers of stained glass windows and lamps choose to portray particular images and to represent certain themes. Her research proposal indicated that she would tape record the interviews she held with individual craftsmen and photograph their creations. Her initial subjects assented to the mechanical means of recording and all went according to plan. When beginning an interview with yet another glassmaker, however, Chapman was taken aback, for the man answered affirmatively when she asked him if he would object to her taping their conversation. She was disturbed even more, she reports, when another man who had overheard the question and response also refused to be taped. "The reason that I was upset over their not wanting to be taped," Chapman writes, "was not so much that they did not want to be recorded, but that up until that time everyone else to whom I had spoken had been taped and I was afraid that in some way this would make these interviews of inferior quality, or even less accurate." Feeling later that her apprehensions were perhaps "a trifle absurd," she also realized, and was appalled at, what had happened to her. "I had allowed my photography and recording to become more than what they were, that being tools," she confesses, adding, "I can remember being more concerned with whether the sound on the tape or the quality of the photographs were good than with what people were saying and showing to me."[16]

Being denied permission to tape record interviews with one of her subjects was also of concern to Ellen Stekert. While gathering the information that served as the basis for her doctoral dissertation, Stekert worked with a Mr. B, a traditional singer in his eighties who had made it known that he wished someone to record the songs he knew before he died. Mr. B had no objections to being taped while he was singing, but he refused to allow Stekert to record their conversations, despite her wish to do so. "Because his actual performance was important to me," writes Stekert, "and as a check on how much the tape machine inhibited him, I had a hidden recording machine with me," the existence of which was unknown to others as well as to Mr. B. Stekert turned on the hidden recorder, she reports, when Mr. B "began to perform folklore materials, or offered information too complex to remember or notate." She adds, in seeming justification for her actions, "These recordings are solely for my private use." One obvious result of using the concealed machine was that Stekert was able to record on tape information that she regarded as essential to her fieldwork aims and that she felt might otherwise have escaped her. Another, and unexpected, result was that she discovered what Alice, the woman with whom Mr. B had lived for thirty years, thought of her and her work. "It was through inadvertently leaving this hidden machine where it recorded Alice and Mr. B at the reunion [of their family], talking about me to a cousin, that I discovered the extent of Alice's hostility to me," writes Stekert. "She said I made a 'damn fool' of myself asking 'foolish questions.' "[17]

The extent to which subjects are unknowingly tape recorded or filmed is difficult to ascertain, given the fact that reported instances of such practices are rare. Fieldworkers who admit to employing the technique usually offer as justifications their desire to document behavior as it occurs "naturally" or to obtain information that subjects might not be willing to disclose if they knew or suspected that their words or actions were being documented mechanically.[18] According to fieldworkers' oral and published reports, however, surprising numbers of subjects readily agree, or are easily persuaded, to allow themselves to be taped or photographed. The reasons for this are not entirely clear, for fieldworkers seldom explain in person or in print just how they broach the subject of taping or filming, how they justify their desire to use a tape recorder or camera, and what they tell subjects the utilization or disposition of sound recordings and photographs or films will be. One result of subjects' consenting to having their words, images, actions, or possessions documented mechanically is that they often expect, ask, or are offered the opportunity to hear the tapes, see or have copies of the photographs, or view the films. If and when such events occur, there is always a variety of human responses, ranging from feelings of flattery or self-satisfaction to those of disappointment or embarrassment, and such responses must also be counted among the results of fieldwork.

Whether fieldworkers' experiences are recorded mentally, in writing, on magnetic tape, on film, or in some combination of these ways, the records serve as sources for any tangible outputs that might be produced to serve as vehicles for communicating to other people the essence of what fieldworkers conceive themselves to have learned as a result of their having observed, interacted with, and queried people at first hand. Books, monographs, periodical essays, and conference papers are the most common outputs of fieldwork; they often include segments of transcribed tape recordings or some photographs (usually of dwellings, noteworthy structures or physical sites, or the most cooperative subjects or informants). Edited tapes or films, and selected sets of photographs or slides, have grown in popularity recently as fieldwork outputs, though they are most often presented as supplements to, rather than as substitutes for, written or published documents. Such tangible products of fieldwork obviously constitute results, but their creation and presentation or dissemination also bring about results in the form of reactions from others and the effects these reactions have upon both fieldworkers and subjects.

As was noted earlier in this work, many (if not most) individuals who engage in fieldwork involving people studying people do so out of necessity rather than by choice. Conducting fieldwork has become a requirement in numerous college and university courses, particularly in the social sciences; and it is often conceived to be an essential *rite de passage* for those seeking advanced degrees and aspiring for admission into, or recognition within, certain professional circles or academic disciplines (such as anthropology, folkloristics, sociology, and ethnomusicology). In addition, as has also been demonstrated, there are always personal motives, as well as scholarly or scientific objectives, for doing fieldwork, and the former can never be subordinated to the latter. Hence, most individuals who conduct fieldwork not only expect, and are expected, to produce some tangible output that documents and informs others about their fieldwork experiences, but they also tend to expect, and to be expected, to produce outputs that will please others (especially their superiors and peers) as well as themselves. Reactions to the tangible outputs of fieldwork, and the effects of these reactions, are usually viewed by fieldworkers and others as more important results of fieldwork than are the outputs themselves, for favorable reactions enhance or perpetuate the fieldworker's relative professional, public, and financial status.

Fieldwork experiences constitute the bases for countless M.A. theses and Ph.D. dissertations in colleges and universities throughout the world; the resultant acceptance of these documents and the awarding of graduate degrees for which they are a prerequisite have greater importance for the individuals concerned than do the theses and dissertations that are the tangible outputs of their fieldwork experiences. Furthermore, information gathered during fieldwork projects designed to fulfill course or degree requirements often provides material for published works or edited films which, when assessed positively, can bring recognition and sometimes even fame or fortune to their creators, with Margaret Mead, Bronislaw Malinowski, Franz Boas, William Foote Whyte, and John Dollard as noted examples. Having done fieldwork and having produced an output does not of itself ensure reward, for the information obtained and selected for presentation, as well as the manner in which the information is communicated, evoke responses and are subject to assessment. Yet whether or not reactions to outputs of fieldwork are positive, there could be no outputs, and thus nothing for others to react to, without the experiences on which they are based.

It is fairly easy to determine the effects of response to fieldwork outputs upon the professional, public, and financial status of their creators. It is more difficult to ascertain subjects' reactions to these outputs and the effects of outputs upon subjects. In many instances, subjects are unaware that their behavior and the information they give fieldworkers are sources and subjects of essays, books, or films. In other cases, subjects know in advance the probable nature of the output, but if it materializes, it is not accessible to them, either because the fieldworker does not provide them with copies or because the subjects do not possess the background, skills, or technology needed to experience, comprehend, appreciate, or assess the output. The contents of a book about their way of life remains a mystery to subjects who are illiterate; a technical monograph on their social structure has little meaning to literate subjects unfamiliar with the analytical constructs and jargon of the anthropologist or sociologist. In recent years, however, the spread of literacy, the growing accessibility of printed matter and audio-visual resources, and the widespread interest in rights and responsibilities in human interrelationships have made large numbers of individuals aware of, familiar with, and concerned about the outputs of fieldwork projects for which they have served as subjects.

That research subjects are often not only aware of fieldwork outputs, but also react to and are affected by them is illustrated by several events that have been described in print since mid-century. In a letter published in 1956 in the anthropological journal, *Man,* for example, Murray Groves writes, "Increasing literacy in English among Melanesians now threatens alien fieldworkers in that area with a new occupational hazard.... One day in 1955 in Port Moresby," Groves reports, "a slight young man stopped me in the street and spoke to me. 'Excuse me, sir. Are you an anthropologist?' he asked. I said that I was. 'Yes, so I understand,' he said, now smiling at me as if we had just shared a delightful secret." Having asked and received answers to his introductory questions, the young man continued. "'You have presumably read Malinowski,' he added. Again I said 'Yes,'" notes Graves. The young man pursued the point. "'Then, sir, you may be interested to know that Malinowski was in error,' the young man said. 'I am a Trobriand Islander myself, and from what I have heard of his writings it is clear that Malinowski did not understand our system of clans and chiefs.'" Groves writes that the young man "then pulled a type-written page of foolscap from his pocket" and stated, "'Here is a short account I have written myself,'" adding, "'It outlines the facts as they really are, and I should like you to have it.'" Groves asked the man what he wished him to do with the document. "'I should be much obliged if you would make the facts available to those who have been misinformed,' the young man answered." Writes Groves, "I promised to do my best for him, and to fulfill that promise I append the statement which he gave me. It was written in English and it is exactly reproduced hereunder. It should be compared with *Argonauts of the Western Pacific,* pp. 62-72." The document, titled "Index of the Permanent Position of Chiefs (Gweguia) in Trobriand Islands," is reproduced following Groves' letter in *Man* and offered, as the young man had requested, as a modern-day Trobriand Islander's attempt to correct what he conceived to be a fieldworker's mistakes about an aspect of Trobriand social structure.[19]

More dramatic is a description in *Human Organization* (summer 1958) of an event staged by irate townspeople in reaction to a book-length work based upon a fieldwork project for which they had served as subjects. Assured when they permitted a research team to study their community that any outputs of the project would neither identify individual citizens nor describe them or their activities disparagingly, the town's residents were outraged when one of the fieldworkers published a book that violated their expectations by doing both. The editorial characterizes the event, which was but one manifestation of the subjects' reaction to fieldwork output:

> A small upstate New York village has now been immortalized in anthropological literature under the name of "Springdale." The local newspaper reports that the experience has not been entirely a pleasing one. We pass on this account:
>
> "The people of the Village [Springdale] waited quite awhile to get even with Art Vidich, who wrote a *Peyton Place*-type book about their town recently.
>
> "The featured float of the annual Fourth of July parade followed an authentic copy of the jacket of the book, *Small Town in Mass Society*, done large-scale by Mrs. Beverly Robinson. Following the book cover came residents of [Springdale] riding masked in cars labeled with the fictitious names given them in the book.
>
> "But the pay-off was the final scene, a manure-spreader filled with very rich barnyard fertilizer, over which was bending an effigy of 'The Author'."
>
> The account suggests that a good time was had by all—on this particular occasion. Nevertheless, local observers report that the disturbance caused by the book in the village has not been entirely compensated for by even such a ceremony carried out in the best anthropological traditions.[20]

The author of the *Human Organization* editorial uses the incident as a basis for raising fundamental questions about fieldwork and its outputs. He poses two specific questions:

1. What obligation does the author of a community study have to the people of the community he studies, particularly when it comes to publication of his findings?
2. When the author is a member of a research team, what obligations does he have to the project director? And what obligations does the project director have to him?[21]

The editorial raises other issues, as do printed responses from the authors of the controversial book and from other social scientists. What is appropriate in identifying individual subjects (by actual or fictitious names) in fieldwork outputs? What kinds of information are permissible for fieldworkers to include in any outputs they create? What rights and responsibilities should determine the nature and specifics of fieldwork outputs of fieldworkers and subjects, on the one hand, and of team fieldwork project directors and individual fieldworkers who participate in team projects, on the other? While no definitive conclusions or specific recommendations are presented in the editorial or in the written responses to it, two fundamental points emerge: (1) that the outputs of fieldwork projects can become known to, evoke reactions from, and have effects upon research subjects; and (2) that the potential effects of fieldwork outputs upon the human beings who are their sources and subjects cannot be subordinated to scientific or scholarly concerns when those outputs are being planned and produced.[22]

While individual subjects often react negatively to or are adversely affected by fieldwork outputs, there are also instances in which subjects react favorably to and benefit from fieldwork outputs which describe them, their behavior, or the information of which they were the sources. Folksinger Huddie Ledbetter (best known by his nickname "Leadbelly"), for example, became well-known throughout the United States and England after John and Alan Lomax, who first recorded his singing and musicmaking in a Lousiana prison in 1933, made the world aware of his artistry. Their belief that Ledbetter was a powerful and unique performer prompted the Lomaxes to appeal to the

governor of Louisiana to pardon the singer. This pardon
enabled Leadbelly to develop (with the aid of the Lomaxes) a
remarkable singing career.[23] Mrs. Zsuzsuánna Palkó, a storyteller admired for her skill as a performer by members of the
small rural community in which she resided, was immortalized
when Linda Dégh described her narrative repertoire and narrat-
ing abilities in print. She was honored by the Hungarian government in 1954, which conferred upon her "the distinguished title
of Master of Folklore," awarded her "3,000 forints (about
$120)," and presented her with a "medal bearing an inscription
which she could not read" at a ceremony in Budapest, the capital city which she had never visited but had often envisioned in
her imagination.[24] Another storyteller, Maryland fisherman
Alex Kellam, was pleased when he received from George Carey,
the fieldworker to whom he had told over one-hundred tales, a
copy of Carey's book in which he was presented as the "star
informant." The publication of the book, moreover, gained
Kellam a reputation in Maryland, as well as invitations to speak
and tell his tales to audiences at local public schools and at the
University of Maryland.[25] Such reactions and effects are results
that neither fieldworkers nor subjects can foresee.

Beyond the diversity of experiences and examples suggested
here, there are results of fieldwork that defy description and
elude exemplification. The friendships made, the feelings evoked
and shared, the human concerns generated and expressed by
those who come to know each other through their involvement
in the enterprise we call *fieldwork* can only be known, understood, and appreciated by the individuals involved. Moreover,
the unpleasant surprises and shattered expectations, the warm
welcomes and hostile receptions, the hopes aroused and promises broken, the mementos treasured and nightmares relived, the
insights gained and the assumptions called into question can
neither be quantified nor articulated succinctly. In one respect,
fieldwork never really ends, neither for fieldworkers nor subjects, for each fieldwork adventure is a part of an ineradicable
continuum of human experience. The results of fieldwork,
therefore, are not ends. What is learned from the experience
results instead in continuities and new beginnings whose ends
are usually unpredictable and indeterminable. Such is the nature
of human relationships and of human beings' constant search
to understand themselves and know each other.

Epilogue

I n this book we have attempted to counter the view, widely held and generally reinforced by conventional fieldwork guides or manuals, that individuals can conduct fieldwork involving people studying people without being human. To be a good and successful fieldworker, it is often felt and stated, one must learn to be detached and objective and to suppress human feelings and concerns that can only interfere with the task at hand. This view, which can be termed the tabula rasa approach to fieldwork, is rooted in good intentions. It makes the neophyte aware that fieldwork is serious business and that the fieldworker's role carries with it the responsibility to contribute new insights, unencumbered by personal bias or selfish motives. But the tabula rasa approach to fieldwork distorts reality by implying that one can forget or temporarily blank out what one knows and has experienced, and that, during the period of encounter with subjects, one can operate in vacuo.

That human beings cannot unlearn what they have learned and forget all that they have experienced (even with effort and for a predetermined period of time) is an indisputable behavioral fact. "After the moment of an observer's birth," writes philosopher Abraham Kaplan, "no observation can be undertaken in all innocence. We always know something already," he states, "and this knowledge is intimately involved in what we come to know next, whether by [purposeful] observation or in any other way."[1] Hence, "no human perception *is* immaculate,'.' as Kaplan so aptly puts it,[2] and what we already know directly affects what we subsequently perceive, learn, and experience.

If we cannot forget or suppress what we know, then we cannot study people without our studies being directed and affected by our behavior as, and our past relationships with, human beings. Yet it seems to be the shared humanity of fieldworkers and subjects that most concerns those who engage in fieldwork and those who provide the instruction (whether in the classroom or in print) for prospective fieldworkers. They feel that by being merely human, and hence at one with their subjects, fieldworkers are not adequately differentiated from subjects and cannot satisfactorily accomplish their research objectives. But apart from individuals' personal motives for doing fieldwork— and the importance of personal motives cannot be overlooked or minimized, as examples throughout this book make clear— the underlying *and* overriding objective of all fieldwork involving people studying people is to better understand the human species. The shared membership of fieldworker and subject in a common species makes it inevitable for them to empathize and impossible for them to relate to each other as if they had no common identity. The ways in which fieldworkers and subjects perceive, conceive, interact with, and react to each other necessarily have precedents in their past experiences as and with human beings. They may differ from each other in skin color, native language, lifestyle, or worldview, but the ways in which they communicate with and learn from each other are rooted in their similarities rather than in their differences.

The experiences of the individuals described and discussed throughout this book emphasize the human element in fieldwork. Those who become involved in fieldwork ventures, whether in the role of fieldworker or subject, are first and foremost fellow human beings. They enjoy the same kinds of advantages and make the same kinds of mistakes that people always enjoy and make. They are both considerate and inconsiderate toward each other. They are supportive and exploitive, sharing and selfish, believing and suspicious, and accurate and incorrect in their inferences about and assessments of each other's behaviors. They love and hate, joke and quarrel, enlighten and deceive, cooperate and compete. It is through their shared humanity that fieldworkers and subjects learn from and teach each other, and this gain in understanding of the species in which they share membership makes fieldwork, with all its human limitations and faults, a worthwhile and satisfying endeavor.

Notes

I: DILEMMAS

1. Frank H. Cushing, "My Adventures in Zuñi," *The Century Illustrated Monthly Magazine,* 25:2 (December 1882), 206. Cushing's three-part article (the latter two installments of which were distinguished with "II" and "III" following the title) in 25:2 (December 1882), 191-207; 25:4 (February 1883), 500-511; and 25:1 (May 1883), 28-47, as well as Sylvester Baxter's essay "An Aboriginal Pilgrimage," which appeared in the same magazine, 24:4 (August 1882), 526-536, were reprinted as *My Adventures in Zuñi* (Santa Fe, N.M.: The Peripatetic Press, 1941), with an introduction by E. DeGolyer. Cushing's characterization of his experiences was reprinted more recently as *My Adventures in Zuñi* (Palmer Lake, Colo.: Filter Press, 1967), with an introduction by Oakah L. Jones, Jr.

2. Ibid., p. 206.

3. Ibid.

4. Ibid., pp. 206-207.

5. Ibid., p. 207.

6. Ibid.

7. Ibid.

8. Answers to some of these questions regarding Boas's fieldwork can be inferred from *The Ethnography of Franz Boas: Letters and Diaries of Franz Boas Written on the Northwest Coast from 1886 to 1931,* ed. Ronald P. Rohner (Chicago and London: University of Chicago Press, 1967); see also Ronald P. Rohner, "Franz Boas: Ethnographer on the Northwest Coast," and " 'Franz Boas Among the Kwakiutl,' Interview with Mrs. Tom Johnson," in *Pioneers of American Anthropology: The Uses of Biography,* ed. June Helm (Seattle and London: University of Washington Press, 1966), pp. 149-212 and 213-222, respectively. Available regarding Benedict's fieldwork is Margaret Mead, *An Anthropologist at Work: Writings of Ruth Benedict* (Boston: Houghton Mifflin Company, 1959), although little can be inferred about the circumstances under which Benedict made her observations.

9. Franz Boas, *Primitive Art,* reprint ed. (New York: Dover Publications, 1955), p. 155.

10. See, for example, Ruth Benedict, "Introduction," *Zuni Mythology,* 2 volumes (New York: Columbia University Press, 1935), I, xi-xiii.

11. Melville J. and Frances S. Herskovits, *Dahomean Narrative: A Cross-Cultural Analysis* (Evanston, Ill.: Northwestern University Press, 1958), p. 6.

12. Colin Turnbull, *The Mountain People* (New York: Simon and Schuster, 1972), pp. 15-17.

13. William Hugh Jansen, "The Reputation of Folktale Performers in American History," in *IV International Congress for Folk-Narrative Research in Athens. Lectures and Reports,* ed. Georgios A. Megas (Athens, 1965), p. 191.

14. John Dollard, *Caste and Class in a Southern Town,* 3d ed. (Garden City, N.Y.: Doubleday and Company, 1957), pp. 9-11, 27, and 32-36.

15. Herbert Gans, *The Levittowners: Ways of Life and Politics in a New Suburban Community* (New York: Random House, 1967), p. 445.

16. See, for example, such manuals as Kenneth S. Goldstein, *A Guide for Field Workers in Folklore* (Hatboro, Pa.: Folklore Associates, 1964); John Lofland, *Analyzing Social Settings: A Guide to Qualitative Observation and Analysis* (Belmont, Calif.: Wadsworth Publishing Company, 1971); James B. Spradley and David W. McCurdy, *The Cultural Experience: Ethnography in Complex Society* (Chicago: Science Research Associates, 1972); William J. Samarin, *Field Linguistics: A Guide to Linguistic Field Work* (New York: Holt, Rinehart, and Winston, 1967); Robert B. Edgerton and Lewis L. Langness, *Methods and Styles in the Study of Culture* (San Francisco: Chandler and Sharp, 1974); and Jan Harold Brunvand, *A Guide for Collectors of Folklore in Utah* (Salt Lake City: University of Utah Press, 1971). This characterization obtains for guides in other disciplines requiring firsthand observations and interviews, such as M. L. Stein, *Reporting Today: The Newswriter's Handbook* (New York: Cornerstone Library Publications, 1971).

17. See, for example, Brunvand, p. 7, and as suggested by the tone in such works as Spradley and Mc Curdy, and Richard M. Dorson, *Buying the Wind: Regional Folklore in the United States* (Chicago and London: University of Chicago Press, 1964), pp. 1-20.

18. Cushing, "Adventures," p. 191.

19. See *Man and Culture: An Evaluation of the Work of Bronislaw Malinowski,* ed. Raymond Firth (London: Routledge & Kegan Paul, 1957); and Bronislaw Malinowski, *A Diary in the Strict Sense of the Term* (New York: Harcourt, Brace, and World, 1967), trans. Norbert Guterman, preface by Valetta Malinowski, and introduction by Raymond Firth, pp. xvii, 106 (note at bottom of page).

20. Margaret Mead, *Blackberry Winter: My Earlier Years* (New York: William Morrow & Company, 1972), p. 194.

21. Henry Glassie, *All Silver and No Brass: An Irish Christmas Mumming* (Bloomington and London: Indiana University Press, 1975), pp. xii and xv.

22. In regard to Kennedy's fate, see Raymond Kennedy, *Field Notes on Indonesia: South Celebes, 1949-50,* ed. Harold C. Conklin (New Haven, Conn.: Human Relations Area Files, 1953), pp. iii, vii, and ix. For information about Rockefeller, see *The Asmat of New Guinea: The Journal of Michael Clark*

Rockefeller, ed. Adrian A. Gerbrands (New York: Museum of Primitive Art, 1967). Reference to the death of his son is made by John T. Hitchcock in "Fieldwork in Gurkha Country," in *Being an Anthropologist: Fieldwork in Eleven Cultures,* ed. George D. Spindler (New York: Holt, Rinehart and Winston, 1970), pp. 169-170. For a list of some who have suffered illnesses, see *Marginal Natives at Work: Anthropologists in the Field,* ed. Morris Freilich (Cambridge, Mass.: Schenkman Publishing Company, 1977), pp. 20-21.

23. Cushing, "Adventures," p. 206.

24. Ibid., p. 192.

25. Ibid., p. 193.

26. Ibid., p. 199.

27. Ibid., p. 200.

28. Ibid., p. 202.

29. Ibid., p. 203.

30. Ibid., p. 204.

31. Ibid., p. 205.

32. Ibid., "Adventures, II," 25:4 (February 1883), 502.

33. Ibid., p. 506.

34. Ibid., p. 509.

35. Ibid., p. 511.

36. Ibid., "Adventures, III," 26:1 (May 1883), 40.

37. Trikoli Nath Pandey, "Anthropologists at Zuni," *Proceedings of the American Philosophical Society,* 116:4 (August 1972), 323.

38. Nancy Oestreich Lurie, "Women in Early American Anthropology," in *Pioneers of American Anthropology: The Uses of Biography,* ed. June Helm (Seattle and London: University of Washington Press, 1966), p. 59.

39. Pandey, "Anthropologists at Zuni," pp. 326, 327.

40. Lurie, "Women in Early American Anthropology," p. 61, quoting correspondence from Matthew W. Stirling.

41. Pandey, "Anthropologists at Zuni," p. 328, n. 40.

42. Lurie, "Women in Early American Anthropology," p. 55.

43. Pandey, "Anthropologists at Zuni," p. 327.

44. Ibid., p. 329.

45. Ibid., p. 330.

46. Ibid., p. 331.

47. Ibid., pp. 331-332.

48. Ibid., p. 332, quoting personal communication from Ruth Bunzel.

49. Ibid., p. 333.

50. Trikoli Nath Pandey, "'India Man' among American Indians," in *Encounter and Experience: Personal Accounts of Fieldwork,* ed. André Béteille and T. N. Madan (Honolulu: University Press of Hawaii, 1975), p. 199, n. 9.

51. Pandey, "'India Man,'" p. 203; see also Pandey, "Anthropologists at Zuni," p. 335, in which it is reported that the man said, "I guess you have people like them in India, too. They are everywhere."

52. Pandey, "Anthropologists at Zuni," p. 330, n. 56.

53. Ibid., p. 335.

54. Pandey, "'India Man,'" p. 206, n. 18.

55. Ibid., p. 203.

56. Ibid., pp. 197, 198.
57. Pandey, "Anthropologists at Zuni," p. 333.
58. Pandey, " 'India Man,' " pp. 199-200.
59. Pandey, "Anthropologists at Zuni," p. 333.
60. Pandey, " 'India Man,' " p. 209.
61. Ibid., p. 206, n. 18.
62. Ibid., p. 206.

II: ALTERNATIVE MEANS, MANY ENDS

1. Margaret Mead, *Blackberry Winter: My Earlier Years* (New York: William Morrow & Company, 1972), p. 137.
2. Ibid.
3. Ibid.
4. Ibid., p. 128.
5. Ibid., p. 129.
6. Ibid., p. 132.
7. Peggy Golde, "Odyssey of Encounter," in *Women in the Field: Anthropological Experiences,* ed. Peggy Golde (Chicago: Aldine Publishing Company, 1970), p. 67.
8. Ibid.
9. Ibid.
10. Ibid., pp. 67-68.
11. Ibid., p. 68.
12. Ibid.
13. Ibid., p. 92.
14. Seymour Martin Lipset, "The Biography of a Research Project: *Union Democracy,*" in *Sociologists at Work: Essays on the Craft of Social Research,* ed. Phillip E. Hammond (New York: Basic Books, 1964), pp. 96-97.
15. Ibid., p. 97.
16. Ibid.
17. Ibid.
18. Ibid.
19. Ibid., p. 98.
20. The results of the research are presented in S. M. Lipset, Martin Trow, and James S. Coleman, *Union Democracy* (Glencoe, Ill.: The Free Press, 1956); reprinted in paperback (Garden City, N.Y.: Doubleday Anchor Books, 1962).
21. James West, *Plainville, U.S.A.* (New York: Columbia University Press, 1945), p. vii.
22. Ibid.
23. Ibid., pp. vii-viii.
24. Ibid., p. viii.
25. Ibid.
26. Ibid.
27. Ibid., pp. viii-ix.
28. Adrian C. Mayer, "On Becoming a Participant Observer," in *Encounter and Experience: Personal Accounts of Fieldwork,* ed. André Béteille

and T. N. Madan (Honolulu: University Press of Hawaii, 1975), p. 29.

29. Ibid.
30. Ibid.
31. Ibid.
32. Ibid.
33. Ibid.
34. Ibid., p. 30.
35. Ibid., p. 31.
36. Ibid.
37. Leela Dube, "Woman's Worlds—Three Encounters," in *Encounter and Experience,* p. 157.
38. Ibid., p. 158.
39. Ibid.
40. Ibid.
41. Ibid.
42. Ibid., p. 159.
43. Ibid.
44. Ibid.
45. Ibid., p. 150.
46. Ibid., p. 159.
47. Ibid.
48. Ibid., p. 160.
49. Ibid.
50. Ibid., p. 164.
51. Helen Codere, "Field Work in Rwanda, 1959-1960," in *Women in the Field,* p. 145.
52. Ibid.
53. Ibid.
54. Ibid.
55. Ibid.
56. Ibid., pp. 145-146.
57. William Foote Whyte, *Street Corner Society: The Social Structure of an Italian Slum,* 2d ed. (Chicago: University of Chicago Press, 1955), p. 280.
58. Ibid.
59. Ibid., p. 281.
60. Ibid., pp. 280-281.
61. Ibid., p. 281.
62. Ibid.
63. Ibid.
64. Ibid., pp. 281-282.
65. Ibid., p. 282.
66. Ibid., p. 283.
67. Ibid.
68. Ibid.
69. Ibid.
70. Ibid.
71. Hortense Powdermaker, *Life in Lesu: The Study of a Melanesian Society in New Ireland* (New York: W. W. Norton and Company, 1933).
72. Hortense Powdermaker, *Stranger and Friend: The Way of an Anthro-*

pologist (New York: W. W. Norton & Company, 1966), p. 131.
73. Ibid.
74. Ibid.
75. Ibid.
76. Ibid.
77. Ibid., p. 132.
78. Ibid.
79. Ibid.
80. Ibid.
81. Ibid., p. 133.
82. Ibid., p. 134.
83. Ibid., p. 136.
84. Ibid.
85. Ibid., p. 137.
86. Ibid.
87. Ibid., pp. 132-133.
88. Ibid., p. 23.
89. Ibid.
90. Ibid.
91. Ibid., p. 24.
92. Ibid.
93. Ibid., p. 33.
94. Ibid.
95. Ibid., p. 133.

III: CONFRONTATION

1. Gladys-Marie Fry, *Night Riders in Black Folk History* (Knoxville: University of Tennessee Press, 1975), p. vii.
2. Ibid., pp. vii-viii.
3. Ibid., p. viii.
4. Napoleon A. Chagnon, *Yanomamö: The Fierce People* (New York: Holt, Rinehart and Winston, 1968), p. 4.
5. Ibid., p. 5.
6. Ibid., pp. 5-6.
7. Marilyn Fithian, "Chapter Seventeen: Personal Impressions and Reactions, Two," in William S. Hartman, Marilyn Fithian, and Donald Johnson, *Nudist Society: An Authoritative, Complete Study of Nudism in America* (New York: Crown Publishers, 1970), p. 302.
8. Ibid., p. 303.
9. Ibid., p. 307.
10. Ibid., p. 308.
11. Ibid.
12. John Lofland, *Analyzing Social Settings: A Guide to Qualitative Observations and Analysis* (Belmont, Calif.: Wadsworth Publishing Company, 1971), p. 93. It is referred to as "incognito interviewing" by Elizabeth Bott in *Family and Social Network: Roles, Norms, and External Relationships in Ordinary Urban Families,* Third Impression (London: Tavistock Publications, 1957, 1968), p. 20.

13. Margaret Mead, *Blackberry Winter: My Earlier Years* (New York: William Morrow & Company, 1972), p. 147.

14. Carla Bianco, *The Two Rosetos* (Bloomington: Indiana University Press, 1974), pp. 219-220.

15. Chagnon, *Yanomamö*, p. 4.

16. R. Lincoln Keiser, "Fieldwork among the Vice Lords of Chicago," in *Being an Anthropologist: Fieldwork in Eleven Cultures*, ed. George D. Spindler (New York: Holt, Rinehart and Winston, 1970), pp. 226-227. See also Ernestine Friedl, "Field Work in a Greek Village," in *Women in the Field: Anthropological Experiences*, ed. Peggy Golde (Chicago: Aldine Publishing Company, 1970), pp. 198-199; Chie Nakane, "Fieldwork in India—A Japanese Experience," in *Encounter and Experience: Personal Accounts of Fieldwork*, ed. André Béteille and T. N. Madan (Honolulu: University Press of Hawaii, 1975), p. 15; William B. Schwab, "Comparative Field Techniques in Urban Research in Africa," in *Marginal Natives at Work: Anthropologists in the Field*, ed. Morris Freilich (Cambridge, Mass.: Schenkman Publishing Company, 1977), p. 49; and Gloria Marshall, "Field Work in a Yoruba Community," in *Women in the Field: Anthropological Experiences*, ed. Peggy Golde (Chicago: Aldine Publishing Company, 1970), p. 171.

17. John Beattie, *Understanding an African Kingdom: Bunyoro* (New York: Holt, Rinehart and Winston, 1965), p. 14.

18. Ibid.

19. Ibid.

20. *The Ethnography of Franz Boas: Letters and Diaries of Franz Boas Written on the Northwest Coast from 1886 to 1931*, ed. Ronald P. Rohner (Chicago and London: University of Chicago Press, 1969), p. 32.

21. Ibid.

22. Ibid., p. 33.

23. Ibid., pp. 33-34.

24. Ibid., p. 34.

25. Ibid.

26. Robert H. Lowie, *Robert H. Lowie, Ethnologist: A Personal Record* (Berkeley and Los Angeles: University of California Press, 1959), p. 60.

27. Herbert Gans, *The Levittowners: Ways of Life and Politics in a New Suburban Community* (New York: Random House, 1967), p. xxiii.

28. Ibid., pp. 441-442.

29. Richard M. Dorson, *Negro Folktales in Michigan* (Cambridge, Mass.: Harvard University Press, 1956), p. 2.

30. Ibid.

31. Ibid., pp. 3-4.

32. Kenneth S. Goldstein, *A Guide for Field Workers in Folklore* (Hatboro, Pa.: Folklore Associates, 1964), pp. 53-54.

33. Lofland, p. 96; see also William Foote Whyte, *Street Corner Society: The Social Structure of an Italian Slum*, 2d ed. (Chicago: University of Chicago Press, 1955), p. 298.

34. Maud Karpeles, *Cecil Sharp: His Life and Work* (Chicago: University of Chicago Press, 1967), pp. 165-166.

35. John Dollard, *Caste and Class in a Southern Town*, 3d ed. (Garden City, N.Y.: Doubleday & Company, 1957), p. 9.

36. Dorson, *Negro Folktales in Michigan*, p. 4.

37. Laura Nader, "From Anguish to Exultation," in *Women in the Field: Anthropological Experiences*, ed. Peggy Golde (Chicago: Aldine Publishing Company, 1970), p. 99.

38. Ibid.

39. Ibid., p. 100.

40. Rohner, *The Ethnography of Franz Boas*, pp. 22-23.

41. William H. Wiser and Charlotte Viall Wiser, *Behind Mud Walls 1930-1960, with a Sequel: The Village in 1970* (Berkeley, Los Angeles, London: University of California Press, 1971), p. 2.

42. Ibid., pp. 1, 3.

43. Ibid., p. 3.

44. Ibid., pp. 5-6.

45. Ibid., p. 6.

IV: CLARIFICATION AND COMPROMISE

1. William Foote Whyte, *Street Corner Society: The Social Structure of an Italian Slum*, 2d ed. (Chicago: University of Chicago Press, 1955), p. 288.

2. Ibid., p. 289.

3. Ibid.

4. Ibid.

5. Ibid.

6. Ibid., pp. 290-291.

7. Ibid., p. 291.

8. Ibid.

9. Ibid.

10. Ibid., p. 292.

11. Ibid.

12. Ibid.

13. Ibid.

14. Ibid.

15. Ibid., pp. 292-293.

16. Ibid., p. 301.

17. Ibid., pp. 321-323.

18. Jean Briggs, *Never in Anger: Portrait of an Eskimo Family* (Cambridge, Mass.: Harvard University Press, 1970), p. 20.

19. Ibid., p. 17.

20. Ibid., pp. 19-20.

21. Ibid., pp. 226-227.

22. Jean Briggs, "Kapluna Daughter," in *Women in the Field: Anthropological Experiences*, ed. Peggy Golde (Chicago: Aldine Publishing Company, 1970), p. 24; a report very similar to the foregoing essay was published by Briggs under the title "Kapluna Daughter: Living with Eskimos," *Trans-Action*, 7:3 (June 1970), 13-24.

23. Briggs, "Kapluna," p. 25.

24. Briggs, *Never in Anger*, pp. 246-247.

25. Ibid., pp. 243-244.

26. Ibid., p. 244.

27. Ibid.
28. Ibid., p. 253.
29. Ibid., p. 254.
30. Ibid., p. 293.
31. Ibid., p. 248.
32. Ibid., p. 265.
33. Ibid., p. 266.
34. Ibid., p. 270.
35. Described by Briggs, ibid., pp. 285-288.
36. Ibid., p. 4.
37. John Dollard, *Caste and Class in a Southern Town,* 3d ed. (Garden City, N.Y.: Doubleday and Company, 1957), p. 1.
38. Ibid., p. 27.
39. Ibid., p. 9.
40. Ibid., p. 10.
41. Ibid., p. 9.
42. Ibid., pp. 10-11.
43. Ibid., pp. 8-9.
44. Ibid., p. 7.
45. Ibid., p. 23.
46. Ibid., pp. 32-33.
47. Ibid., p. 33.
48. Ibid.
49. Ibid., pp. 35-36.
50. Ibid., p. 36.
51. Ibid., p. 38.
52. Ibid., pp. 38-39.
53. Ibid., p. 39.
54. John A. Hostetler and Gertrude Enders Huntington, "The Hutterites: Fieldwork in a North American Communal Society," in *Being an Anthropologist: Fieldwork in Eleven Cultures,* ed. George D. Spindler (New York: Holt, Rinehart and Winston, 1970), p. 200.
55. Ibid., p. 213.
56. Ibid., p. 214.
57. Ibid.
58. Ibid.
59. Ibid.
60. Ibid.
61. Ibid., p. 215.
62. Ibid.
63. Ibid.
64. Ibid.
65. Ibid., pp. 215-216.
66. Ibid., p. 216.
67. Ibid.
68. Ibid., p. 217.
69. Ibid.
70. Ibid.
71. Ibid.

72. Ibid.
73. Leon Festinger, Henry W. Riecken, and Stanley Schachter, *When Prophecy Fails* (Minneapolis: University of Minnesota Press, 1956), pp. 25-30.
74. Ibid., pp. 30-31.
75. Ibid., p. 238.
76. Ibid., pp. 238-239.
77. Ibid., p. 237.
78. Ibid., p. 239.
79. Ibid., p. 240.
80. Ibid.
81. Ibid.
82. Ibid., p. 241.
83. Ibid., pp. 241-242.
84. Ibid., p. 241.
85. Ibid., p. 242.
86. Ibid.
87. Ibid., pp. 243-246.
88. Ibid., pp. 243, 252.

V: REFLECTION AND INTROSPECTION

1. Elliot Liebow, *Talley's Corner: A Study of Negro Streetcorner Men* (Boston and Toronto: Little, Brown and Company, 1967), pp. 232-233.
2. Ibid.
3. Robert K. Dentan, "Living and Working with the Semai," in *Being an Anthropologist: Fieldwork in Eleven Cultures,* ed. George D. Spindler (New York: Holt, Rinehart and Winston, 1970), p. 105.
4. Edward Norbeck, "Changing Japan: Field Research," in *Being an Anthropologist,* p. 264.
5. Norbeck, pp. 263-264; Dentan, p. 105; Alan R. Beals, "Gopalpur, 1958-1960," in *Being an Anthropologist,* p. 55; and Jeremy F. Boissevain, "Fieldwork in Malta," in *Being an Anthropologist,* p. 68.
6. John T. Hitchcock, "Fieldwork in Gurkha Country," in *Being an Anthropologist,* p. 181.
7. Norma Diamond, "Fieldwork in a Complex Society: Taiwan," in *Being an Anthropologist,* p. 122.
8. Jean Briggs, *Never in Anger: Portrait of an Eskimo Family* (Cambridge, Mass.: Harvard University Press, 1970), p. 229.
9. Bronislaw Malinowski, *A Diary in the Strict Sense of the Term* (New York: Harcourt, Brace, and World, 1967), trans. Norbert Guterman, preface by Valetta Malinowski, and introduction by Raymond Firth, pp. xv, xvii, 109-135.
10. *The Ethnography of Franz Boas: Letters and Diaries of Franz Boas Written on the Northwest Coast from 1886-1931,* ed. Ronald P. Rohner (Chicago and London: University of Chicago Press, 1969), pp. 110-114, 125-132.
11. Margaret Mead, *Blackberry Winter: My Earlier Years* (New York: William Morrow & Company, 1972), p. 156.

12. *Marginal Natives at Work: Anthropologists in the Field,* ed. Morris Freilich (Cambridge, Mass.: Schenkman Publishing Company, 1977), p. 21; Aram A. Yengoyan, "Open Networks and Native Formalism: The Mandaya and Pitjandjara Cases," in *Marginal Natives at Work,* pp. 231-232, 251.

13. Ernestine Friedl, "Field Work in a Greek Village," in *Women in the Field: Anthropological Experiences,* ed. Peggy Golde (Chicago: Aldine Publishing Company, 1970), pp. 195-205.

14. Ibid., p. 206.

15. Ibid., pp. 206-207.

16. Ibid., p. 207.

17. Ibid.

18. Colin M. Turnbull, *The Mountain People* (New York: Simon and Schuster, 1972), p. 226.

19. Ibid., pp. 226-227.

20. Ibid., p. 227.

21. Ibid.

22. Ibid., pp. 227-228.

23. Ibid., p. 228.

24. Hortense Powdermaker, *Stranger and Friend: The Way of an Anthropologist* (New York: W. W. Norton & Company, 1966), p. 111.

25. Ibid.

26. Ibid., p. 112.

27. Ibid., pp. 112-113.

28. Ibid.

29. Ibid., p. 116.

30. Ibid.

31. Ibid.

32. Bruce Giuliano, Kathie O'Reilly, and Bari Polonsky, "Those Are My Shoes, It Must Be Me," unpublished paper, on file in the Archive of California and Western Folklore, Center for the Study of Comparative Folklore and Mythology, University of California, Los Angeles.

33. Ibid., p. 7.

34. Ibid., pp. 21-22.

35. Ibid., pp. 25-26.

36. Ibid., p. 30.

37. Ibid.

38. Rohner, *The Ethnography of Franz Boas,* pp. 24-25; for some other examples, see pp. 53, 55, 158, 163, 165, 166.

39. Robert H. Lowie, *Robert H. Lowie, Ethnologist: A Personal Record* (Berkeley and Los Angeles: University of California Press, 1959), p. 10.

40. Rohner, *The Ethnography of Franz Boas,* p. 61.

41. Napoleon A. Chagnon, *Yanomamö: The Fierce People* (New York: Holt, Rinehart and Winston, 1968), p. 10.

42. Ibid.

43. Ibid., p. 11.

44. Ibid.

45. Ibid.

46. Ibid., pp. 11-12.

47. Herbert Gans, *The Levittowners: Ways of Life and Politics in a New*

Suburban Community (New York: Random House, 1967), pp. 447-448. Somewhat related are the remarks by Paul Rabinow, *Reflections on Fieldwork in Morocco* (Berkeley, Los Angeles, London: University of California Press, 1977), pp. 38-39, 73, 75, 94-95.

48. Norbeck, "Changing Japan," pp. 256-257.

49. Ibid., p. 257.

VI: RESULTS

1. Jerry Hyman's characterization of his experiences was set forth in an unpublished essay on the potlatch and excerpted at some length, but without full bibliographical citation, by Myron Glazer in *The Research Adventure: Promise and Problems of Field Work* (New York: Random House, 1972), p. 89.

2. Ibid.

3. Ibid., pp. 89-90.

4. Ibid., p. 90.

5. Ibid.

6. Ibid., p. 91.

7. Ibid.

8. Ibid.

9. Ibid., p. 92.

10. Ibid., pp. 92-93.

11. Richard M. Dorson, *Buying the Wind: Regional Folklore in the United States* (Chicago and London: University of Chicago Press, 1964), pp. 9-10; Kenneth S. Goldstein, *A Guide for Field Workers in Folklore* (Hatboro, Pa.: Folklore Associates, 1964), pp. 130-131.

12. See, for example, Goldstein, pp. 166-173.

13. Goldstein, pp. 87-90. See also Kenneth S. Goldstein, "The Induced Natural Context: An Ethnographic Folklore Technique," in *Essays on the Verbal and Visual Arts, Proceedings of the 1966 Annual Spring Meeting of the American Ethnological Society,* ed. June Helm (Seattle and London: University of Washington Press, 1967), pp. 1-6.

14. Goldstein, *A Guide,* p. 90.

15. Kenneth S. Goldstein, "Experimental Folklore: Laboratory vs. Field," in *Folklore International: Essays in Traditional Literature, Belief, and Custom in Honor of Wayland Debs Hand,* ed. D. K. Wilgus (Hatboro, Pa.: Folklore Associates, Inc., 1967), pp. 74-81.

16. Mary Anne Chapman, "View Through Some Colored Glass," unpublished paper, on file in the Archive of California and Western Folklore, Center for the Study of Comparative Folklore and Mythology, University of California, Los Angeles, pp. 9-10.

17. Ellen J. Stekert, "Two Voices of Tradition: The Influence of Personality and Collecting Environment upon the Songs of Two Traditional Folksingers," unpublished dissertation, University of Pennsylvania, 1965, pp. 73-74.

18. Besides Stekert's experience with concealed mechanical recording equipment, mention is made of the employment of that technique in the fol-

lowing works: Dorson, pp. 15-16; Linda Dégh and Andrew Vazsonyi, "Legend and Belief," in *Folklore Genres,* ed. Dan Ben-Amos (Austin and London: University of Texas Press, 1976), p. 103.

19. Murray Groves, "Trobriand Island Clans and Chiefs," in "Correspondence," *Man, A Monthly Record of Anthropological Science,* 56:189-191 (November 1956), 164.

20. "Editorial: Freedom and Responsibility in Research: The 'Springdale' Case," *Human Organization,* 17:2 (Summer 1958), 1.

21. Ibid., p. 1.

22. Ibid., pp. 1-2. Replies to the editorial appear in the same journal, 17:4 (Winter 1958-1959), 2-7.

23. *The Leadbelly Legend: A Collection of World-Famous Songs by Huddie Ledbetter,* ed. John A. Lomax and Alan Lomax (New York: Folkways Music Publishers, Inc., 1959 and 1965), p. 6.

24. Linda Dégh, *Folktales and Society: Story-Telling in a Hungarian Peasant Community,* trans. Emily M. Schossberger (Bloomington and London: Indiana University Press, 1969), pp. 178-188.

25. George Carey, "The Storyteller's Art and the Collector's Intrusion," in *Folklore Today: A Festschrift for Richard M. Dorson,* ed. Linda Dégh, Henry Glassie, Felix J. Oinas (Bloomington: Indiana University Press, 1976), pp. 87-89.

EPILOGUE

1. Abraham Kaplan, *The Conduct of Inquiry: Methodology for Behavioral Science* (San Francisco: Chandler Publishing Company, 1964), pp. 132-133.

2. Ibid., p. 131.

Index